Safeguarding Children from Abroad

Refugee, Asylum Seeking and Trafficked Children in the UK

Edited by Emma Kelly and Farhat Bokhari

Foreword by Brigid Daniel

Jessica Kingsley *Publishers*
London and Philadelphia

Figure 2.1 reproduced with permission of The London Safeguarding Children Board.

First published in 2012
by Jessica Kingsley Publishers
116 Pentonville Road
London N1 9JB, UK
and
400 Market Street, Suite 400
Philadelphia, PA 19106, USA

www.jkp.com

Library of Congress Cataloging in Publication Data
A CIP catalog record for this book is available from the Library of Congress

British Library Cataloguing in Publication Data
A CIP catalogue record for this book is available from the British Library

ISBN 978 1 84905 157 6
eISBN 978 0 85700 559 5

Printed and bound in Great Britain

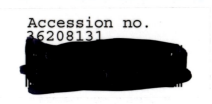
Safeguarding Children from Abroad

Best Practice in Working with Children Series

Edited by Brigid Daniel, Professor of Social Work, Department of
Applied Social Science, University of Stirling

The titles in the Best Practice in Working with Children series are written for the multi-agency professionals working to promote children's welfare and protect them from harm. Each book in the series draws on current research into what works best for children, providing practical, realistic suggestions as to how practitioners in social work, health and education can work together to promote the resilience and safety of the children in their care. Brigid Daniel is Professor of Social Work in the Department of Applied Social Science at the University of Stirling. She is co-author of several textbooks and practice resources on childcare and protection. She was a member of the multi-disciplinary team that carried out a national ministerial review of child protection practice in Scotland.

other books in the series

Making Sense of Child and Family Assessment
How to Interpret Children's Needs
Duncan Helm
Foreword by Brigid Daniel
ISBN 978 1 84310 923 5

Safeguarding Children Living with Trauma and Family Violence
Evidence-Based Assessment, Analysis and Planning Interventions
Arnon Bentovim, Antony Cox, Liza Bingley Miller and Stephen Pizzey
Foreword by Brigid Daniel
ISBN 978 1 84310 938 9

Safeguarding Children in Primary Healthcare
Edited by Julie Taylor and Markus Themessl-Huber
Foreword by Brigid Daniel
ISBN 978 1 84310 652 4

Safeguarding Children and Schools
Edited by Mary Baginsky
Foreword by Brigid Daniel
ISBN 978 1 84310 514 5

Child Neglect
Practice Issues for Health and Social Care
Edited by Julie Taylor and Brigid Daniel
Foreword by Olive Stevenson
ISBN 978 1 84310 160 4

Contents

Foreword

This book reminds us of one of the universal needs of children and young people – the need for a secure attachment relationship that offers age-appropriate nurture, care, encouragement, support and love. The loss of, or separation from a key attachment figure is known to be one of the most traumatic and damaging human experiences that can impact throughout life. By advocating for the use of the term 'separated' children to describe a range of ways in which children and young people end up alone in the UK this book foregrounds this basic human need. In particular, the book draws on attachment theory to analyse the ways in which children and young people may bring with them patterns of insecure attachment that are likely to impact on their formal and informal relationships once here.

The children and young people who find themselves in the UK, for whatever reason, without a parent or carer are thus humanised in this book. We are reminded that they have the same developmental needs as all children and young people. At the same time these fundamental, universal needs are overlaid with additional needs because of their experiences in their countries of origin, during the journey here and once in the UK. The needs of each individual will therefore be very different – each young person will have their own powerful story to tell.

This book is aimed at all practitioners who may encounter separated children and young people – which could mean any number of disciplines and professions in any, and all, of child and adult services. The children and young people may directly seek help in their own right, but they are more likely to come to the attention of someone in a position to help if practitioners are curious and interested enough to notice their needs.

The book is highly practical and combines theoretical insight with clear advice and guidance. The legislative context is described in detail, including information about Scotland, and there is much information about how the legislation can be used to underpin the provision of help for these young people. It is such a complex area that a clear exposition of the policy and legislative context is invaluable.

The book also addresses, head on, some of the problematic areas, most notably issues of age determination. This is a fraught area for practitioners and can deflect attention away from the basic fact that one is faced with an individual who is in need of support. The process of age assessment is carefully explained here. Another fraught area, that is also dealt with sensitively and clearly, is that of return of children and young people to their country of origin.

The book also explores the ways in which separated children and young people's sense of security can be enhanced by having a supported place to live, being listened to and receiving appropriate mental health care. If we can provide these children and young people with the kind of support, encouragement and empathic care that they need, we will maximise the chances of them being able to settle, flourish and make their own contribution to the rich diversity of the UK.

Brigid Daniel,
Professor of Social Work,
University of Stirling, UK

Introduction

Emma Kelly and Farhat Bokhari

Throughout the UK, practitioners are working with children from abroad who are alone in the country. In some areas such work has become almost routine, reflecting the large numbers of children from abroad, whereas in others, only one or two such children are encountered every year. Skills and knowledge therefore range from well-developed expertise with teams and specialist professionals dedicated to safeguarding children from abroad to individual practitioners developing an independent knowledge base, often relying on the internet (Kelly 2009) to respond to new issues and needs. This book offers detailed information for anyone who may work to safeguard and promote the welfare of children from abroad.

Separated children

Previously, we have lacked the language to describe the wide range of children that arrive from abroad in the UK. Only a few of these children will be unaccompanied asylum seeking children (UASC); many others will enter the UK accompanied and then be abandoned or be cared for by a 'stranger', and other children will be from elsewhere in the European Union (EU). In mainland Europe the term 'separated children' is used to describe this diverse group of children and it is a term that the UK would do well to adopt. A separated child is:

> under 18 years of age, outside their country of origin and separated from both parents, or their previous legal, or customary primary caregiver. Some children are totally alone while others, who are also the concern of the SCEP, may be living with extended family members who are not necessarily their customary or primary caregivers. All such children are separated children and entitled to international protection under a broad range of international and regional instruments. (SCEP 2010, p.3)

The Separated Children in Europe Programme (SCEP), established by the United Nations High Commissioner for Refugees (UNHCR) and International Save the Children Alliance, was established in 1998 and introduced its *Statement of Good Practice* in 1999. This statement is based on the United Nations Convention on the Rights of the Child (UNCRC) and the UNHCR's (1997) *Guidelines on Policies and Procedures in Dealing with Unaccompanied Children Seeking Asylum* (see Halvorsen 2002). In the statement it establishes that:

> The SCEP uses the word 'separated' rather than 'unaccompanied' because it more accurately defines the essential problem that such children face. Namely, that they lack the care and protection of their parents or primary caregiver and as a consequence suffer socially and psychologically from this separation. (SCEP 2010, p.4)

The value of this definition is that it can be applied to all children from abroad who are in the UK and are for whatever reasons not being cared for by their primary caregivers. For too long there has been confusion and uncertainty about separated children. Misconceptions abound that all children from abroad need to claim asylum or that all victims of child trafficking must also be asylum seekers. In addition, there is confusion among academics and practitioners as to how to describe such children, with terms such as refugee, migrant and asylum seeker used indiscriminately. With this narrow focus on the circumstances of children from abroad, other groups of children remain hidden, both literally and in terms of professional representation. Using the term 'separated children' gives a name and space to these children and we use it throughout this book.

The term separated children covers all groups of children who may end up in the UK, including UASC, victims of trafficking, children who are migrants but not seeking asylum (such as EU children), children who are accompanied into the UK but become separated after arrival, including those who end up in private fostering situations and those who entered with their parents but have been left in the UK following an unsuccessful family claim for asylum. The SCEP suggests that there are three main categories of children who are likely to be described as separated 'those seeking protection (including asylum), those who have been trafficked and those who are migrants including those seeking family reunification, or economic or education opportunities' (SCEP 2010, p.15).

Importantly, the term separated children does not have any unfavourable associations, unlike that of asylum seeker or victim of human trafficking. Research has shown that UASC actively seek to resist the label of 'asylum seeker' because of the institutional and social discrimination they experience as a result (Chase 2010; Kohli 2006). Other work with trafficked children illustrates how meaningless that term is to most victims of human trafficking; indeed, even within professional spheres there remains a debate about distinctions between trafficked and smuggled young people (Beddoe 2007; Kelly 2009; Pearce, Hynes and Bovarnick 2009). In our experience, it is all too easy for organisations to be seduced by the need to label separated children for the purposes of service provision; whereas a broader focus and one which emphasises these children's separation from primary caregivers should lead to a refocusing on their needs.

The term separated children also innately recognises the potential vulnerability of such children, because they are away from their primary caregivers. It has long been recognised that children who are cared for away from home are vulnerable. As Utting (1997) noted, children cared for away from home are without parental supervision; they may already have been abused or exploited or may lack the 'defence' or understanding to know what is happening, and they are less likely to be taken seriously or may be in isolated circumstances. Although this list of 'vulnerabilities' was written in relation to citizen children, it equally applies to separated children. In addition, separated children may also have had traumatic experiences in their country of origin or in transit; they are in a new country and may not speak English or may not understand the social support systems available. They have lost all contact with anyone and anything familiar to them. This is not to position separated children as 'victims' in need of our protection but to recognise the complex experiences that they are faced with.

Given the range of experiences that separated children are likely to have had before they arrive in the UK, it seems extraordinary that many will receive a lesser service from statutory services than citizen children. Indeed, organisational discrimination has long been noted by those working with separated children (Crawley 2006; Dennis 2002). Much of this stems from the tensions that exist between immigration control and child support and protection. Despite clear domestic policy and procedures as well as international obligations, many separated children continue to find that their status as being subject to immigration control takes precedence over their needs and rights as children. The SCEP is clear in relation to the principle of non-discrimination for separated children:

> All separated children are entitled to the same treatment and rights as national children. They must be treated as children first and foremost whether or not they hold relevant travel, entry, or residence documents, or whether they are perceived

to be in transit. All considerations relating to their immigration status must be secondary and anchored in the principles of child welfare. (SCEP 2010, p.7)

In addition to the belief that separated children have a right to be children first and foremost, there are a number of other principles which have shaped the contributions to this book; namely the right of separated children to be heard, their rights to have decisions made with them in their 'best interests' and the central role of multi-agency working. The voice and the needs of the child underpin all the chapters, as we have taken the position that listening and taking into account the wishes and feelings of separated children is essential. Building on the UNCRC principles, the importance of meaningful participation is made explicit:

The views and wishes of separated children must be sought and taken into account whenever decisions affecting them are being made. Measures must be put in place to facilitate their meaningful participation in line with their age and maturity. (SCEP 2010, p.8)

Additionally, some of the real and potential obstacles in ensuring meaningful participation are identified:

Appropriate safeguards must be put in place to ensure that consultations and interviews do not cause harm to the child. Cultural and linguistic factors, which may serve as a barrier to participation must be addressed. Separated children are entitled to be heard directly or via their legal representative or guardian in any legal procedure. Separated children should always be enabled and encouraged to voice their views, concerns and complaints regarding their care and guardianship, education, health services, legal representation and durable and secure solutions. (SCEP 2010, p.8)

Some of the other challenges that separated children and practitioners may encounter in ensuring meaningful participation are explored throughout the book.

A core UNCRC principle underlying all work to safeguard separated children is the primacy of the 'best interests' of the child. Drawing on this principle the SCEP states:

The best interests of the child must be a primary consideration in all actions concerning every separated child. Any determination or assessment of best interests must be based on the individual circumstances of each child and must consider the child's family situation, the situation in their country of origin, their particular vulnerabilities, their safety and the risks they are exposed to and their protection needs, their level of integration in the host country, and their mental and physical health, education and socio-economic conditions. These considerations must be set within the context of the child's gender, nationality as well as their ethnic, cultural and linguistic background. The determination of a separated child's best interests must be a multi-disciplinary exercise involving relevant actors and undertaken by specialists and experts who work with children. (SCEP 2010, p.6)

Therefore, 'best interests' approach can be seen to represent the need to work holistically with children in assessing and meeting their needs in the short and longer term.

The centrality of multi-agency work in protecting the best interests of a child as identified by SCEP is also a key theme in the chapters that follow. This is acknowledged in government policy (DCSF 2010; Scottish Office 1998; Welsh Assembly Government 2006) as a core approach to effective practice to safeguard and promote the welfare of all children in the UK. This means practitioners need to ensure equality of access to services by separated children. Lord Laming's inquiry into the death of Victoria Climbié (a separated child) highlighted how effective joint working and 'equal access to services of the same quality' for children whatever their background or culture is key to their protection (Laming 2003, p.346).

The chapters in this book explore the identities and journeys of the growing number of separated children in the UK. The contributions reflect the broad range of professionals that are likely to be involved in the care and protection of a separated child including: a social worker and service manager, practitioners from non-governmental organisations (NGOs), a barrister, consultant psychiatrists and a representative from Scotland's Commissioner for Children and Young People (SCCYP) as well as several academics. Each of the chapters examines in depth a core issue for professionals working with separated children. It is hoped that the complexity of the policy and practice in each of these areas is presented in a way that enables practitioners to build on their own understandings. The impact of policy on separated children is examined through case studies or quotes from young people, with the aim of offering practice-based solutions to current difficulties in practice. In addition, all the chapters explicitly comment on the safeguarding needs of separated children, with many making reference to knowledge and process that is familiar to practitioners in their day-to-day work with children in need.

The policy framework for separated children in the UK is complex given that it is a combination of domestic childcare law, national asylum policy and influenced by international obligations. Farhat Bokhari (Chapter 1) provides an overview of the policy and legislative framework that affects all separated children. Bokhari outlines some of the more specific areas of policy and legislation as they pertain to various groups of separated children, including unaccompanied asylum seeking and trafficked children.

The identification of separated children, including when and how, is of central importance in safeguarding. Drawing on extensive social work experience, Philip Ishola (Chapter 2) describes the processes for identifying separated children. Detailed guidance is also given through a case study analysis of the identification of trafficked children with specific reference to the *London Safeguarding Trafficked Children Toolkit*. This multi-agency toolkit has been piloted nationally and is now available as best practice guidance to all practitioners (London SCB 2011).

Linked to identification is the issue of age assessments; if a young person is not recognised to be a child, he or she will not be eligible for support from children's services, education or child health services. Heaven Crawley (Chapter 3) examines the process of age assessments as undertaken by children's services and the processes that a separated child may be subject to by the United Kingdom Border Agency (UKBA). The development of case law that guides best practice in age assessments is examined as well as recent unimplemented proposals to develop regional assessment centres. Much of the chapter is based on the substantial research undertaken by Heaven Crawley into the issue of age assessments in the UK (Crawley 2007).

The provision of accommodation for separated children is dependent on the outcome of an age assessment and even now some local authority areas are still not offering suitable accommodation for minors. Beginning with an exploration of the rights of separated children to accommodation, Hannah Pearce (Chapter 4) explores the particular issues around the provision of accommodation for trafficked children, which includes accompanied or unaccompanied children and European Economic Area (EEA) children. Two of the key questions posed are why do so many of these children go missing and what can be done to prevent this. Examples from current best local authority practice in the UK are discussed as a way of sharing what is currently known to safeguard trafficked children.

The numbers of separated children living in private fostering arrangements is increasingly being recognised. Catherine Shaw and Savita de Sousa (Chapter 5) outline the current legal and policy framework in relation to private fostering in the UK. They highlight the particular challenges and dilemmas facing local authorities and practitioners in identifying, assessing and supporting separated children living with private foster carers, and the potential risks to children if these challenges are not overcome. Possible solutions and practice responses are considered, drawing on major research carried out by the National Children's Bureau (NCB) and the British Association for Adoption and Fostering (BAAF) by the authors and supplemented with practice examples provided by BAAF.

Ruth Reed and Mina Fazel (Chapter 6) explore the well-being and mental health needs of separated children with a focus on factors leading both to resilience as well as mental health problems. Reed and Fazel outline the current literature on the subject and then concentrate on key issues with practice examples. The important role that stable external support can play for these children, in particular in the school environment, as well as the crucial role social services and third sector organisations play are explored. In addition, the safeguarding concerns for this group are raised, in particular, how to ensure that their needs are addressed as well as ensuring that their best interests are supported in an appropriate framework.

Nadine Finch (Chapter 7) considers the legality of proposals to return some separated children to their country of origin, mainly boys from Afghanistan. Finch explores the basis upon which the return of separated children to their country of origin would be lawful in the context of the UNCRC and the EU Returns Directive and compares the UK response with developments in Northern Europe. Finch highlights how the UK returns policy in question is largely immigration led, with little evidence of a child's rights perspective or primacy given to the best interests of the child in such decisions. Interesting concepts of 'adequacy' and 'best interests' are examined in relation to the return of children, including the need to give due consideration to their integration in the host country and an independent assessment of reception conditions to judge the durability of returns.

Rooted in a child's rights perspective, Emma Kelly (Chapter 8) reviews the literature from UK and Europe on what separated children have to tell us about their experiences. These experiences include pre-departure, during transit and arrival and adaptation to life in the UK. Kelly considers why the voices of some separated children are 'unheard', such as migrant and trafficked children, as well as what we can learn about improving services based on the wealth of literature about unaccompanied asylum seeking children's voices.

Stefan Stoyanov (Chapter 9) explores current gaps in upholding the rights of separated children in the UK by introducing independent guardians for this vulnerable group. Scotland is leading the way with its current piloting of a model of guardianship for all separated children. Guardians for separated children are a key requirement of the SCEP and there have long been demands from UK-based NGOs to introduce guardians in UK practice. Guardians are also required by the Council of Europe Convention on Action against Trafficking in Human Beings, ratified by the UK, to protect the best interests of separated children as soon as they are identified.

It is hoped that the core themes of the book cut across national differences in domestic childcare law so that it will be of use to practitioners in Wales, Scotland and Northern Ireland. It is always challenging to adequately reflect the different frameworks and policy attitudes to children in the four nations of the UK, while presenting a detailed analysis of practice. Given that most of the authors are based in England, the book does reflect, in the main, English childcare law and practice, although efforts have been made throughout to acknowledge key legislative differences across the UK. Much of the book is, however, about the practice implications resulting from immigration law, which is a non-devolved matter.

Some of the key areas of difference for practitioners in Wales and Scotland are worth considering, because it can be argued that they represent a more child-rights orientated approach than England. Both nations receive adults (including young people who have been erroneously assessed as over 18) and families through the National Asylum Support Service (NASS) process of dispersal. The dispersal cities of Cardiff, Swansea, Newport, Wrexham and Glasgow are where most separated children are likely to be found, although research shows that separated children are living elsewhere across these nations, including in rural areas (Kelly 2009; SCCYP and Perth 2011). In addition, both Wales and Scotland receive separated children through their sea and airports and they are then referred on to the nearest local authority service.

Wales has adopted an inclusive model in relation to separated children, which links in to the Welsh Assembly's commitment to upholding the UNCRC in all policy and law making. This is enshrined in the Welsh Assembly Government 'Getting it Right' Action Plan of 2009 and the Rights of Children and Young Persons (Wales) Measure in 2010. As well as local areas of expertise, the Welsh Assembly funds a national post of Refugee Advice and Children's Information Officer (Kelly 2009), which stemmed in part from the extensive research that has been undertaken in

Wales into the needs of separated children (Hewett *et al.* 2005; Save the Children 2008).

The Scottish government is also committed to the principles of UNCRC, as seen in its current piloting of the guardianship model. Other key differences for separated children in Scotland stem from the Children (Scotland) Act 1995 whereby local authorities' duties to care for and accommodate a child extend only until the child is 16 years old, although Section 26 of the Act requires that children up to the ages of 18 are safeguarded and their welfare promoted. This has resulted in 'an ambiguity of what persons in that particular age bracket can legally do or not do in Scotland at that age, as well as complicating the issues of agency and consent' (SCCYP and Perth 2011, p.49). Earlier research into UASC in Scotland commented on the geographical distribution of separated children:

> Whilst it is likely that the concentration of refugee communities in Glasgow has acted as a magnet for agents and thus many unaccompanied asylum seeking children have been brought to the city, there are unaccompanied asylum-seeking children under local authority care in other locations in Scotland. (Hopkins and Hill 2006, p.19)

Initial research into child trafficking in Scotland suggests that most victims were identified in Glasgow (Rigby 2009; Save the Children Scotland 2006) but more recently child victims have been found in Aberdeen as well as other areas outside of Glasgow (SCCYP and Perth 2011).

Inevitably, there are areas of practice that are not covered in this book. In particular, issues concerning intercultural communication and use of interpreters are only briefly touched on. The dearth of literature on migrant and EU children who end up in the UK is evident throughout. It should also be noted that the contents of this book in no way replace the need for specialist legal advice for separated children; on matters relating to the immigration status of separated children, it is essential that a reputable lawyer is consulted.

Conclusion

This book explores a wide range of current challenges confronting separated children upon their arrival into the UK, but crucially also discusses best practice to promote the welfare and rights of this group of children, which is what sets it apart from other material on the subject. It considers the predicament of the whole spectrum of separated children, whether they are UASC, trafficked or migrant children, by focusing on their commonalties and drawing out distinctions where these exist in law, policy or practice. Above all the book is premised on a children's rights perspective with an appreciation of their experiences as central to safeguarding without discrimination. It is hoped that the information presented here will serve as a useful resource for practitioners, policy makers, academics and students, as well as being accessible to a wider non-specialist audience.

References

Beddoe, C. (2007) *Missing Out: A Study of Child Trafficking in the North-West, North- East and West Midlands.* London: ECPAT UK.

Chase, E. (2010) 'Agency and silence: Young people seeking asylum alone in the UK'. *British Journal of Social Work 40,* 7, 2050–2068.

Crawley, H. (2006) *Child First, Migrant Second: Ensuring That Every Child Matters.* London: Immigration Law Practitioners' Association.

Crawley, H. (2007) *When is a Child Not a Child? Asylum, Age Disputes and the Process of Age Assessments.* London: Immigration Law Practitioners' Association.

Dennis, J. (2002) *A Case for Change: How Refugee Children in England are Missing Out.* London: Refugee Council.

Department for Children, Schools and Families (DCSF) (2010) *Working Together to Safeguard Children: A Guide to Inter-agency Working to Safeguard and Promote the Welfare of Children.* Nottingham: DCSF.

Halvorsen, K. (2002) 'Separated children seeking asylum: The most vulnerable of all'. *Forced Migration Review 12,* 7, 35–37.

Hewett, T., Smalley, N., Dunkerley, D. and Scourfield J. (2005) *Uncertain Futures: Children Seeking Asylum in Wales.* Cardiff: Save the Children.

Hopkins, P. and Hill, M. (2006) *'This Is a Good Place to Live and Think about the Future': The Needs and Experiences of Unaccompanied Asylum-Seeking Children and Young People in Scotland.* Glasgow: Scottish Refugee Council.

Kelly, E. (2009) *Bordering on Concern: Child Trafficking in Wales.* Swansea: Children's Commissioner for Wales and ECPAT UK.

Kohli, R. (2006) 'The sound of silence: Listening to what unaccompanied asylum seeking children say and do not say'. *British Journal of Social Work 36,* 5, 707–721.

Laming, L. (2003) *The Victoria Climbié Inquiry: Report of an Inquiry.* London: HMSO.

London Safeguarding Children Board (SCB) (2011) *London Safeguarding Trafficked Children Toolkit.* London: London SCB.

Pearce, J., Hynes, P. and Bovarnick, S. (2009) *Breaking the Wall of Silence: Practitioners' Responses to Trafficked Children.* University of Bedfordshire and NSPCC.

Rigby, P. (2009) *Child Trafficking in Glasgow: Report of a Social Work Case File Analysis of Unaccompanied Asylum Seeking Children.* Glasgow: Child Protection Committee.

Save the Children (2008) *The Care and Protection of Asylum-seeker and Trafficked Children in Wales: Agenda for Action.* Wales: Save the Children. Accessed on 2 June 2011 at www.wsmp.org.uk/documents/wsmp/Asylum%20Seeking%20Children/Reports/Agenda%20for%20Action.eng.Dec.08.pdf

Save the Children Scotland (2006) *A Hidden Trade: Child Trafficking Research in Scotland.* Glasgow: Save the Children Scotland.

Scotland's Commissioner for Children and Young People (SCCYP) and Perth UHI (2011) *A Scoping Study into the Nature and Extent of Child Trafficking in Scotland.* Edinburgh: SCCYP.

Scottish Office (1998) *Guidance Protecting Children – A Shared Responsibility: Guidance on Inter-Agency Co-operation in Scotland.* Edinburgh: Scottish Office.

Separated Children in Europe Programme (SCEP) (2010) *Statement of Good Practice: Separated Children in Europe Program,* 4th edn. Denmark: Save the Children.

United Nations High Commissioner for Refugees (UNHCR) (1997) *Guidelines on Policies and Procedures in Dealing with Unaccompanied Children Seeking Asylum.* Geneva: UNHCR.

Utting, W. (1997) *People Like Us: The Report of the Review of the Safeguards for Children Living Away from Home.* London: The Stationery Office.

Welsh Assembly Government (2006) *Safeguarding Children: Working Together Under the Children Act 2004.* Cardiff: Welsh Assembly.

Chapter One

Separated Children in the UK

Policy and Legislation

Farhat Bokhari

Introduction

Many thousands of separated children travel to the UK every year for a variety of reasons. A proportion of these children seek asylum, but an unknown number remain a hidden population. They may be fleeing countries in conflict or in economic and political instability, escaping abusive families or being exploited by human traffickers. The majority of separated children settle in neighbouring countries, particularly during times of political upheaval in their own country, and only some undertake the longer and often dangerous journeys required to reach countries like the UK (SCEP 2010). The clandestine nature of their travel and entry into the UK coupled with strict border controls has resulted in them being forced to travel in what can be potentially life-threatening conditions (Burgess 2009). Their journey does not end with their arrival into the UK, since many of them still have to navigate a path through the maze of asylum and immigration law before they can face a future of safety and stability.

Policies aimed at asylum seekers, including separated children who apply for asylum, increasingly focus on barriers to keep them out and discourage them from leaving their countries in the first place (Bloch 2000; Hassan 2000). This exclusionary focus has created tensions between policy, particularly immigration and asylum policy, and the UK's domestic law relating to children and its international obligations to consider the best interests of all children, no matter what their immigration status. It has been argued that this tension has allowed inconsistent and inadequate support to be provided to separated children (Dennis 2002). In addition, a 'culture of disbelief' has become entrenched at all levels of practice, whereby separated children who apply for asylum are not always seen as vulnerable children but thought to be adult (18 years old and over) economic migrants seeking entry to the UK to expropriate benefits from the social welfare system (Bhabha and Finch 2006; Crawley 2007).

This chapter explores what it means to be a separated child and why this is a useful term to describe certain groups of children. It also provides an overview of the overarching policy and legislative framework that affects all separated children. Specific areas of policy and legislation are examined as they pertain to various groups of separated children, including unaccompanied asylum seeking and trafficked children.

Defining separated children

According to the Separated Children in Europe Programme, separated children are defined as those who are under 18 years of age and may be separated from both parents or a 'customary primary caregiver' (SCEP 2010, p.3). This means that those children arriving in the UK with an adult, who is not their parent or customary primary caregiver, are also separated children. Being separated from their legal carers makes these children extremely vulnerable and potentially at risk of being exploited and/or abused by the accompanying adult(s) or others. In the UK the term 'separated children' has not been used widely because of a narrower immigration led focus on asylum seeking children. The Home Office, the department responsible for immigration, uses the term 'unaccompanied asylum seeking child' (UASC) to define a child under 18 years of age who is applying for asylum in his or her own right and who is separated from both parents and not being cared for by an adult who by law or custom has that responsibility. However, UASC is not considered a useful term since it leaves out children who are accompanied by unrelated adults with no legal or customary responsibility for them as well as children who are not applying for asylum.

It is difficult to ascertain the exact numbers of separated children in the UK because of inconsistencies in definition and identification procedures used by agencies. The Home Office (HO) and United Kingdom Border Agency (UKBA) record figures for asylum seeking children; more recently the Child Exploitation and Online Protection Centre (CEOP) has analysed the numbers of trafficked children in the UK. However, they have faced challenges in collecting data on children who are harder to detect upon entry and remain invisible in the statistics. These hidden children include some living with an undocumented immigration status or in private fostering situations (Ayotte 2000; Bokhari and Kelly 2010). There were 2985 children claiming asylum on their own in 2009 (*The Guardian* 2010) and possibly some of these were among the 287 trafficked children known to have entered the UK between March 2009 and February 2010 (CEOP 2010). It is important to treat these figures with caution as they may represent the tip of the iceberg, given the clandestine nature in which many separated children enter the UK and remain hidden while in the country (CEOP 2010).

What is known about these children is that they generally fit into certain groups (these often overlap), which explain the reasons why and how they become separated. These categories include refugee and asylum seeking children, trafficked children who may be exploited before, during or after their journey, and migrant children travelling on their own initiative or sent abroad by their families. What is common to them all is their desire for safety, stability and a better life abroad. By law some separated children, irrespective of their immigration and asylum status, become the concern of the local authority children's social services whose duty it is to provide them with accommodation, education and help accessing other services while their immigration status is being determined (Free 2005). Crawley (2007, 2010) has cautioned against using western conceptions of childhood and distinguishing between 'deserving' and 'undeserving' categories, where economic migrants are considered to belong to the latter category. Instead she calls for understanding the rights and needs of all groups of separated children and the larger national and global picture when framing national policies and procedures. Crawley (2010) shows that in practice separated children's accounts about their journeys are often not listened to nor do those assessing their status or eligibility for services always understand their political maturity or independence.

In a comparison of statistics between 2002 and 2004, Bhabha and Finch (2006) show that separated children, mainly asylum seeking, belong to the age range of 16 to 17 years, with the next largest group being 14 to 15 years old. Boys tend to outnumber girls in the asylum statistics, even though the number of girls claiming asylum has grown over the years. However, the reverse is true for children trafficked into the UK, where the overwhelming majority are girls aged between 14 and 17 years old (CEOP 2010).

Separated children come to the UK from a wide variety of countries, the majority being countries experiencing conflict or some kind of upheaval or human rights abuses against certain groups. Asylum figures show that Afghanistan, Iraq and Somalia have featured consistently on the top of the list since 2002 (Bhabha and Finch 2006). The most recent child trafficking figures place Vietnam, Nigeria and China as the main source countries, with increasing numbers of Roma children being trafficked to the UK

(CEOP 2010). Interestingly, if the statistics are broken down by age and gender, they reveal different patterns of asylum seeking. It is observed that more children as compared to adults seek asylum from particular countries and that more girls may seek asylum from different countries compared to adults or boys (Bhabha and Finch 2006). This statistical evidence points to the existence of child and gender-specific forms of persecution and abuse and the importance of understanding the context and patterns of migration when undertaking assessments.

The overwhelming majority of separated children who need to make an application for asylum do so after entering the UK rather than at ports of entry (Crawley 2007). This may demonstrate that some children are entering the UK clandestinely and are not picked up by immigration authorities at ports of entry. Alternatively, they may enter with a 'friend', that is as an accompanied minor, and it is not until later that they are abandoned or found in unsafe situations that they need to make a claim for asylum. Other children may be abandoned by human smugglers after their entry into the UK with the smugglers being paid only to ensure they enter the country. Trafficked children, on the other hand, whether accompanied or unaccompanied, remain exploited by and under the control of their trafficker while in the UK. Some trafficked children are instructed by their trafficker(s) to apply for asylum, only to disappear from local authority accommodation while their asylum claim is being determined (Beddoe 2007). Girls with EU passports showing them as adults and with the right to visa-free travel into the UK are met by traffickers upon their arrival and completely escape the immigration radar (Beddoe 2007), although there is an increased vigilance at ports. In addition, privately fostered children enter the UK accompanied by a distant relative or unrelated adult mainly on short-term visitor visas and may remain undocumented (and vulnerable to potential abuse) unless the adult registers it as a private fostering situation within 28 days, or if the child comes to the attention of social services through neighbours or other authorities (BAAF 2006).

Legal and policy framework

Both childcare legislation and asylum and immigration legislation apply to separated children in the UK. Although childcare law primarily regulates the care and protection of children, research indicates that immigration control often takes precedence in decisions with implications for the level of support available to separated children (Kelly 2009). While immigration law is applicable UK wide, domestic law on children is determined at a national level so there are variations in childcare law between England,

Wales, Scotland and Northern Ireland. The English government *Working Together to Safeguard Children* policy acknowledges that children entering the UK are potentially the most vulnerable and in greatest need and calls for a multi-agency approach to ensure better coordination and responsiveness in safeguarding them (DCSF 2010).

The United Nations Convention on the Rights of the Child (UNCRC) (United Nations 1989) was ratified in the UK in 1991, but has not explicitly incorporated it into domestic UK law, including asylum and immigration law (Brownlees and Finch 2010). Article 3 of the UNCRC obligates ratifying States to treat the best interests of the child as a primary consideration in all decisions affecting the child. Article 12 emphasises the participation of separated children in decisions, which can be facilitated by legal advocates for them. Until November 2008, the UK had a general reservation on Article 22 of the UNCRC in relation to children subject to immigration control, as regards their entry, stay and departure from the UK, which has been frequently criticised by the UNCRC monitoring body and children's rights agencies in the UK. This reservation has been at the root of the tension between immigration and local authority social services departments on policies related to children subject to immigration control, where it has contributed to the exclusion of this category of children from the services and protection to which they are entitled under domestic childcare law and UNCRC obligations. A direct consequence of the removal of this reservation is that the government now has to ensure that the UNCRC rights of children subject to immigration control are fully implemented on the same basis as citizen children by all agencies with duties to safeguard children (Bolton 2011).

Childcare policy and legislation

The overarching policy in relation to safeguarding and protecting children is set out in the Children Act 1989 and is further extended in the Children Act 2004. Under the Children Act 1989 for England and Wales and the Children (Scotland) Act 1995 local authorities are legally bound to safeguard and promote the welfare of children in their care and provide support to children, irrespective of their immigration status or nationality. Section 17 (1) (a) of the Children Act 1989 states that every local authority shall have the general duty 'to safeguard and promote the welfare of children within their area who are in need'. The Children Act 1989 goes on to define a child in need as one who has a disability or whose standard of development or health would not be achieved or maintained or would deteriorate without social services support. This legislation makes clear that separated children have the same rights as citizen children to accommodation, financial and other support and protection. Furthermore, the principles underlying the Children Act 1989 require that the welfare of the child be the paramount consideration in court decisions affecting the child and that the wishes of the child and his or her autonomy as an individual be respected (Brayne and Carr 2010). This echoes the principles of the UNCRC, which calls for the best interests of the child to be the primary consideration in decisions affecting a child's future. Similarly, Section 11 of the Children Act 2004 requires that most English public bodies with responsibility for children also have regard to safeguard and promote the welfare of children in their care. Section 28 of the Act requires agencies in Wales to do the same.

Additionally, the Children Act 2004 is also relevant to separated children in that its focus on safeguarding children through multi-agency partnership work is necessary to meet the wide ranging needs of separated children who may come into contact with many agencies. The inquiry led by Lord Laming (Department of Health and Home Office 2003) into the death of Victoria Climbié was the impetus for the Children Act 2004 and its provisions for multi-agency working and local safeguarding children boards (LSCBs) to coordinate the actions of key agencies working with children. However, until recently concern was expressed by the exclusion from compulsory participation of the Immigration Service, National Asylum Support Service (NASS) and detention centres – all of which have significant contact with separated children, particularly asylum seeking children (Crawley 2007). With the advent of the UK Borders Act 2007, UKBA is now required to adhere to a Code of Practice to keep separated children safe from harm (UKBA 2008). This includes a commitment to greater participation in LSCBs or their equivalent in Scotland, Child Protection Committees.

Accommodation

Section 20 (1) of the Children Act 1989 provides for accommodation and support for children in need who have no adult with parental responsibility for them, are lost or abandoned, or their caregiver is prevented from caring for or accommodating the child (Brayne and Carr 2010). Similar support is provided to UASC under Section 25 of the Children (Scotland) Act 1995. This section provides children with a higher level of support and has been named as the preferred pathway for supporting separated children as clarified by legal precedent in the Hillingdon Judgment 2003 (Refugee Council 2007) and government guidance in the LAC Circular 13 (Department of Health 2003). Upon reaching 18 years of age, some of these children would automatically be supported under the Children (Leaving

Care) Act 2000, which amends the Children Act 1989, and was put in place to ensure a better transition to adulthood. However, those who reach their 18th birthday and are from the European Economic Area (EEA) do not have this automatic entitlement, because they are excluded by Section 54 of the Nationality, Immigration and Asylum Act 2002. The Children (Leaving Care) Act 2000 imposes duties on local authorities towards children who have been 'looked after' (who enter care under 16 years of age) and categorises former looked after children as 'eligible', 'relevant', 'former relevant' or 'qualifying' in order to work out the services they are entitled to. These children are generally provided with accommodation with foster parents or in residential care or other supervised accommodation with regular reviews to assess their changing needs.

However, problems arise for children whose asylum claims have not been decided by the time they turn 18 years of age because they then become the responsibility of the NASS and are dispersed (bar a few exceptions) to areas outside of London, thus breaking up their support networks. Asylum seekers dispersed by NASS may end up anywhere in the UK, including the northwest, midlands and northeast of England, Wales and Scotland.

It has been the practice of some local authority children's services to class separated children as 'children in need' under Section 17 of the Children Act 1989, the Children (Scotland) Act 1995 and the Children (Northern Ireland) Order 1996 (Ayotte and Williamson 2001). Research has documented how many separated children are placed in semi-independent accommodation, especially after the age of 16 (Crawley 2006). These children are often highly vulnerable individuals who have lived through traumatic experiences and leaving them without appropriate care is likely to hinder their development and expose them to exploitation. In particular, research (Beddoe 2007) has found that trafficked children placed in unsuitable accommodation can easily be traced by traffickers and tend to go missing soon after being placed there. According to the Hillingdon Judgment 2003, Section 17 of the Children Act 1989 is primarily meant to provide support for children and their families and although it can be used to provide accommodation to separated children, it is not recommended given their higher support requirements (Refugee Council 2007). Furthermore, only 'looked after' children under Section 20 are entitled to leaving care services once they reach 18 years of age and if they have been in care for 13 consecutive weeks or more, from 13 years of age upwards. Therefore, separated children supported under Section 17 will not be eligible for any form of leaving care support.

Despite the potential protection afforded by childcare law, practitioners cite a lack of resources and funding by the government as a major impediment to their being able to offer comprehensive support to separated children. In order to avoid the costs of a leaving care service, local authorities may provide accommodation to separated children under Section 17 of the 1989 Act (Joint Committee on Human Rights 2007). In contrast to citizen children who are care leavers, separated children have limited access to funding for benefits unless they have refugee status or discretionary leave to remain. Separated children whose ages are disputed by the Home Office also have restricted rights to accommodation and support. Children's social care practitioners have identified this discrepancy in funding as discriminatory towards separated children (Ayotte and Williamson 2001; Brownlees and Finch 2010).

Private fostering

The British Agency for Adoption and Fostering believes that there are thousands of unknown privately fostered children in the UK and that many of them are likely to be separated children (BAAF 2006). Some communities have traditionally sent their children abroad to be brought up by distant relatives or friends in order to improve their own and their families' prospects, and while this can be a positive experience, it also potentially places these children in vulnerable situations (Bokhari and Kelly 2010). Under the Children Act 1989, Section 67 (1), it is the duty of all local authorities to safeguard all children being privately fostered in their area and ensure that information has been given to people in the area about private fostering regulations. The Act defines private fostering as a situation where a child under the age of 16 (or under 18 if the child has a disability) is placed privately for more than 28 days in the care of someone who is not the child's guardian or close relative.

It is the fostering adults' responsibility to inform the local authority about a fostering arrangement lasting more than 28 days within 48 hours of the child's arrival or before the child arrives. BAAF has expressed concerns over the small number of notifications and children mainly coming to the attention of social services by accident or reporting by neighbours (Bokhari and Kelly 2010). The Children Act 2004 (Section 44) and the Children (Private Arrangements for Fostering) Regulations 2005 are aimed at strengthening the notification and regulation system of private fostering (Crawley 2006).

Asylum and immigration policy and legislation

UK immigration law and policy is complex and changes frequently. Its complexity is partly derived by EU and European Commission regulations and directives and international conventions that the UK is obliged to abide by. In the main, UK asylum and immigration law is based on the Convention Relating to the Status of Refugees 1951 (ratified by the UK) and its Protocol 1967, which set out the rights of refugees and the protections to which they are entitled. The Refugee Convention 1951 recognises that people cannot return to their country of origin because of a well-founded fear of persecution for reasons of race, nationality, membership of a particular social group, religion or political opinion. It has been suggested that not all groups of separated children, for example trafficked children, should be expected to make an asylum claim but rather be allowed residency as a victim of trafficking.

Since 2006 the Home Office began a UASC Reform Programme and published *Better Outcomes: The Way Forward* in 2008, setting out its vision of immigration and asylum policy over the next few years (Home Office 2008). Under Section 55 of the Borders, Citizenship and Immigration Act 2009, UKBA is now required to have regard to safeguard and promote the welfare of children in the UK. It is a similar duty as that placed on other agencies under Section 11 of the Children Act 2004. Crawley (2010) argues that the Home Office reform programme is premised on the assumption that most separated children are not genuine asylum seekers but abusers of the system. In 2009 UKBA also produced a Code of Practice that critics argue does not make enough reference to the UNCRC, nor does it mention a guardian for children or clarify age assessment procedures (ILPA 2009).

Separated children's immigration status

In 2005, the UK government announced a five-year plan on asylum and immigration entitled *Controlling our Borders: Making Migration Work for Britain* (HM Government 2005), which led to the development of a New Asylum Model (NAM) to expedite asylum cases and the passage of the Immigration, Asylum and Nationality Bill 2005. Some aspects of NAM have been welcomed, such as the single case owner, but the timescale to process cases continues to be a concern (Refugee Council 2007). The Scottish Refugee Council (2009) has called for a review of the timescale and for the introduction of an independent advocate, called a guardian. The Immigration, Asylum and Nationality Bill 2005 allows children with refugee status only temporary rights to remain in the UK until they are

17½ years old (Refugee Council 2005). The Refugee Council (2005) has stressed how this determination is counterproductive in that it negates the spirit of the Refugee Convention while creating uncertainty and instability in the lives of refugee children.

Separated children who make a claim for asylum can expect to have a number of determinations made about their immigration status. Provided they meet the criteria set down by the Refugee Convention 1951, they can be recognised as a refugee. They have proved a well-founded fear of persecution under the terms of the Refugee Convention and been given indefinite leave to remain in the UK. If separated children are recognised as refugees, they will be given indefinite leave to remain in the UK, although only for an initial five-year period. After which they are required to reapply and depending on whether it is safe for them to return, another judgment is made. According to the Refugee Council (2007), only small numbers of children are granted refugee status and the majority are granted after appeal.

Children can also be allowed to stay in the UK on humanitarian protection grounds, granted if the child has been refused refugee status but the Home Office decides that it is unsafe for the child to return to his or her country of origin. It is granted for five years or less, and at the end of it the Home Office reviews the situation before deciding on another determination. Not many separated children receive this level of protection (Free 2005).

Separated children are more likely to be granted discretionary leave to remain in the UK if there are no safe reception arrangements in their country of origin and they do not apply for refugee status or humanitarian leave. The Home Office home country reports determine whether or not there are safe reception arrangements in place; however, a range of issues need to be considered such as locating the family and assessing whether they are receptive to the child being returned. Services such as Family Tracing from the Red Cross and the international assessment service provided by Families Across Borders can help with this decision-making process. Under new Home Office policy, children can now be given discretionary leave only up to the age of 17½ years (Home Office 2008). After this age, children can reapply with the help of their care professional. However, even with discretionary leave, there are problems in terms of age assessments preventing decisions in favour of the child.

Age assessments

A significant number of separated children claiming asylum have their age disputed by the Home Office and/or local authority social services (Crawley 2007). The consequences of being judged as an adult include going through adult immigration procedures and being 'dispersed', being accommodated with adults, and possibly being detained and fast tracked out of the UK.

It is difficult to verify a child's chronological age with any certainty and this is acknowledged by UNHCR's (1997) *Guidelines on Policies and Procedures in Dealing with Unaccompanied Children Seeking Asylum*. The Merton Judgment, following a case between R (B) v London Borough of Merton, has established what is known as 'Merton-compliant' age assessments, which require a range of factors to be considered by children's services before arriving at an age determination (Children's Legal Centre 2003). In relation to trafficked children, Article 10 of the Council of Europe Convention on Action against Trafficking in Human Beings (COE) requires that the benefit of the doubt be given to a child whose age is disputed. It states: 'when the age of the victim is uncertain and there are reasons to believe that the victim is a child, he or she shall be presumed to be a child and shall be accorded special protection measures pending verification of his/her age' (Council of Europe 2005, p.11). This applies to all authorities including police, immigration and local authority children's services. This means that when there are concerns about trafficking and the child states that they are under 18, they must be given the benefit of the doubt and receive services as a child until age can be proved.

Returns

Some separated children, though not EEA citizens or children subject to Dublin II Regulation, are entitled to apply for asylum and regularise their immigration status through UK asylum and immigration law. Central to the Refugee Convention is the principle of non-refoulement – not returning any individual to persecution. The Nationality, Immigration and Asylum Act 2002 prohibits the removal of an asylum seeking child from the UK while his or her asylum application is being determined and if a negative determination is made not without ensuring adequate reception arrangements exist. However, under the third country rule as stated in Section 33 and Schedule 3 of the Asylum and Immigration (Treatment of Claimants) Act 2004, a separated child who has claimed asylum in another EU country, and is without a parent in the UK, can be returned to the original country of asylum. The Dublin II Regulation outlines the mechanisms to quickly determine the EU Member State responsible for examining an asylum application by a non-EU country national and his or her transfer to that State. This is part of the drive to harmonise asylum policies among EU Member States and focuses on the control of asylum seekers rather than on their protection needs (Refugee Council 2007).

Anti-trafficking policy and legislation

The main international anti-trafficking law that has provided an internationally accepted definition of trafficking is the United Nations (2000) *Protocol to Prevent, Suppress and Punish Trafficking in Persons, Especially Women and Children, Supplementing the United Nations Convention against Transnational Organized Crime*, commonly known as the Palermo Protocol. Article 3(c) states that 'the recruitment, transportation, transfer, harbouring or receipt of a child for the purpose of exploitation shall be considered "trafficking in persons" even if this does not involve any of the means set forth in subparagraph (a) of this article'. The means referred to include threats, coercion, abduction, fraud and deception among others. Simply put, the definition states that the movement of a child for exploitation is trafficking, irrespective of his or her consent. A more comprehensive protection and prevention framework is provided by the COE, ratified by the UK in 2008 (Bokhari 2008). The COE reiterates the definition of child trafficking as stated in the Palermo Protocol, which makes clear that children's consent to their own exploitation is not possible and thus their consent is considered immaterial and they are to be treated as a victim of the crime of human trafficking, which has been legislated against by the UK.

In line with the Palermo Protocol and the COE, the UK has amended existing legislation to create the offence of human trafficking. Thus, the Sexual Offences Act 2003 in England and Wales criminalises trafficking for sexual exploitation into, within or out of the UK. The equivalent Scottish provisions are contained in the Criminal Justice (Scotland) Act 2003. Similarly, the Asylum and Immigration (Treatment of Claimants, etc.) Act 2004 makes it an offence to traffic for exploitation, including forced labour and the removal of organs. Although providing some exceptions, the Act also makes it an offence to attend an asylum interview without valid immigration documents. The Scottish Refugee Council (2009) has been campaigning against this requirement given the context and circumstances of separated children's journeys.

This anti-trafficking legislation is complemented by the UK government's *Action Plan on Tackling Human Trafficking*, last updated in 2009, which covers areas of prevention, law enforcement and protection. This Action Plan, which covers all of the UK, promised the creation of a system of national referral of trafficking cases through authorities charged with the identification of victims of trafficking, including children. The COE uses the concept of 'competent authorities' (one of whom is UKBA) to describe those who come into contact with trafficked children and have decision making powers (Anti-Trafficking Monitoring Group 2010). In 2009 the UK established a multi-agency coordination system called the National Referral Mechanism (NRM) to identify and refer trafficked children for support through the competent authorities. A year later the performance and composition of the NRM was criticised by a number of specialist anti-trafficking organisations (Anti-Trafficking Monitoring Group 2010). In particular, it was criticised for duplicating the role of identification and referral of trafficked children as opposed to adults when this was something already performed by local authority children's services, which also possessed the expertise and statutory duty to safeguard children.

Guardian

The complexity and ever changing nature of asylum and immigration law and its interrelationship with childcare law makes it difficult to imagine separated children on their own being able to make the right decisions leading to positive outcomes for them. This recognition has been behind the drive by various NGOs in the UK to appoint an independent guardian for separated children (Pearce, Hynes and Bovarnick 2009). The SCEP (2010) notes the necessity of guardians in a range of areas from ensuring best interest decisions to best practice in service provision. With regard to child trafficking, Article 10 (4) (a) of the COE requires States to set up a 'legal guardian, organisation or authority, which shall act in the best interests of that child as soon as a separated child is identified as a victim'.

Human Rights Act 1998

Although not as frequently utilised, the UK Human Rights Act 1998 includes provisions that can protect the rights of separated children where these are being undermined by government policies or local authority practice. The Human Rights Act 1998 incorporates the European Convention for the Protection of Human Rights and Fundamental Freedoms 1950 (ECHR) into UK law.

The following articles of the Act can be used to strengthen a separated child's claim for discretionary leave to remain in the UK. These articles are: the right to life (Article 2), prohibition of torture and inhuman, degrading treatment (Article 3), rights to liberty and security (Article 5) and respect for family life and privacy (Article 8) (Ayotte and Williamson 2001). By virtue of this Act, cases seeking a remedy for a breach of ECHR rights can now be tried in the UK courts, whereas before it came into force in October 2000, such cases would have had to be taken to the European Court of Human Rights in Strasbourg. This can still be done as a last resort.

Migrant children

The United Nations Convention against Transnational Organized Crime and its Protocol against the Smuggling of Migrants by Land, Sea and Air (2000), ratified by the UK in 2006, is focused on preventing and criminalising the smuggling of migrants. It defines 'smuggling' as the illegal transport of a person or persons across state borders for financial or material benefit to the smuggler. The Convention does note in Article 3 (a) and (b) that those who are smuggled could be in danger and face degrading treatment or exploitation.

Separated children who have no claim to asylum and may not be victims of exploitation are an underrepresented group in research literature and policy in relation to how best to support this group. These children are usually undocumented and often classed as 'illegal' entrants, even if their entry may have been legitimate but they failed to apply to regularise their stay. For all its complexity, practitioners still find it simpler to guide asylum seeking children but struggle to assist undocumented migrant children (Brownlees and Finch 2010). Some practitioners have used Article 8 of the Human Rights Act 1998 to apply for discretionary leave by establishing a child's sense of family and permanence in the UK, which would be severely disrupted should they have to leave. This underdeveloped area requires greater engagement by agencies, academics and policy makers to consider child welfare and protection within a framework that acknowledges children's autonomy and considers broader questions about global economic inequalities and migration (Dottridge 2008).

Conclusion

This chapter has demonstrated the complexity in accessing support and services for separated children arriving in the UK. Much of the legislation and policy assumes that separated children are largely asylum seeking children. Child migrants choosing to travel to the UK for a better life, trafficked children and children in private fostering situations remain a hidden group that local authority children's services struggle to assist (Brownlees and Finch 2010; Shaw *et al.* 2010). Even asylum seeking children whose rights are more clearly established in law find their stories disbelieved, their age questioned and little attention given to their need to understand and participate in decisions affecting their future. These are some of the reasons why an independent guardian representing the best interests of children in the process of regularising their status in the UK is considered crucial. However, UK childcare law and policy is in a much stronger position to represent the best interests of separated children, whatever their nationality or background. The impact of the relatively recent removal of the reservation to the UNCRC and the introduction of a child safeguarding duty on UKBA remains to be seen. To achieve the goal that every child matters, the UK would need to fully adopt the UNCRC provisions into its legislation so that children's rights, including their right to participation and the primacy of their best interests, becomes a concern for all agencies relevant to children's welfare and protection (Brownlees and Finch 2010).

References

Anti-Trafficking Monitoring Group with Dottridge, M. (2010) *Wrong Kind of Victim. One Year On: An Analysis of UK Measures to Protect Trafficked Persons.* London: Anti-Slavery International for the Anti-Trafficking Monitoring Group.

Ayotte, W. (2000) *Separated Children Coming to Western Europe: Why They Travel and How They Arrive.* London: Save the Children.

Ayotte, W. and Williamson, L. (2001) *Separated Children in the UK: An Overview of the Current Situation.* London: Save the Children, Refugee Council.

Beddoe, C. (2007) *Missing Out: A Study of Child Trafficking in the North-West, North-East and West Midlands.* London: ECPAT UK.

Bhabha, J. and Finch, N. (2006) *Seeking Asylum Alone Unaccompanied and Separated Children and Refugee Protection in the UK.* Harvard: Macarthur Foundation.

Bloch, A. (2000) 'A new era or more of the same? Asylum policy in the UK'. *Journal of Refugee Studies* 13, 1, 29–42.

Bokhari, F. (2008) 'Falling through the gaps: Safeguarding children trafficked into the UK'. *Children and Society 22*, 3, 201–211.

Bokhari, F. and Kelly, E. (2010) 'Child Rights, Culture and Exploitation – Learning from UK Experiences of Child Trafficking.' In G. Craig (ed) *Child Slavery Now.* Bristol: Policy Press.

Bolton, S. (2011) 'Best Interests': Safeguarding and Promoting the Welfare of Children.' In S. Bolton, K. Kaur., S. S. Luh, J. Peirce and C. Yeo (eds) *Working with Refugee Children: Current Issues in Best Practice.* London: ILPA.

Brayne, H. and Carr, H. (2010) *Law for Social Workers.* Oxford: Oxford University Press.

British Association for Adoption and Fostering (BAAF) (2006) Submission of Evidence to the Home Affairs Select Committee. Accessed on 19 October 2010 at www.baaf.org.uk/info/lpp/pf/hacom.pdf

Brownlees, L. and Finch, N. (2010) *Levelling the Playing Field.* London: UNICEF.

Burgess, K. (2009) 'Children smuggled into Britain are overwhelming the UK Border Agency'. *The Times* 23 May 2009. Accessed on 3 May 2001 at www.timesonline.co.uk/tol/news/politics/article6345636.ece

Child Exploitation and Online Protection Centre (CEOP) (2010) *Strategic Threat Assessment: Child Trafficking in the UK.* London: CEOP.

Children's Legal Centre (2003) *Information Note on The Queen on the Application of B v Merton London Borough Council [2003] EWHC 1689 (Admin), [2003].* Accessed on 31 May 2011 at www.childrenslegalcentre.com/Resources/CLC/Documents/PDF%20A-M/Merton%20Note.pdf

Council of Europe (2005) *Convention on Action against Trafficking in Human Beings.* Warsaw: COE.

Crawley, H. (2006) *Child First, Migrant Second: Ensuring that Every Child Matters.* London: Immigration Law Practitioners' Association.

Crawley, H. (2007) *When is a Child Not a Child? Asylum, Age Disputes and the Process of Age Assessment.* London: Immigration Law Practitioners' Association.

Crawley, H. (2010) '"No one gives you a chance to say what you are thinking": Finding space for children's agency in the asylum system'. *Area 42*, 2, 162–169.

Dennis, J. (2002) *A Case for Change: How Refugee Children in England are Missing Out.* London: Refugee Council.

Department for Children, Schools and Families (DCSF) (2010) *Working Together to Safeguard Children. A Guide to Inter-agency Working to Safeguard and Promote the Welfare of Children.* London: TSO.

Department of Health (2003) *Local Authority Circular (2003) 13: Guidance on Accommodating Children In Need and their Families.* London: Department of Health.

Department of Health and Home Office (2003) *The Victoria Climbié Inquiry: Report of an Inquiry by Lord Laming.* London: TSO.

Dottridge, M. (2008) *Kids Abroad: Ignore Them, Abuse Them or Protect Them. Lessons on How to Protect Children on the Move from Being Exploited.* Geneva: Terres des Hommes International Foundation.

Free, E. (2005) *Young Refugees: A Guide to the Rights and Entitlements of Separated Refugee Children.* Glasgow: Save the Children.

Guardian, The (2010) 'Where do child asylum seekers to the UK come from?' 8 June. Accessed on 20 July 2011 at www.guardian.co.uk/news/datablog/2010/jun/08/child-asylum-seekers-data-uk

Hassan, L. (2000) 'Deterrence measures and the preservation of asylum in the United Kingdom and United States'. *Journal of Refugee Studies 13*, 2, 184–204.

HM Government (2005) *Controlling our Borders: Making Migration Work for Britain.* London: TOS.

Home Office (2008) *Better Outcomes: The Way Forward. Improving the Care of Unaccompanied Asylum Seeking Children.* London: Home Office (BIA).

Immigration Law Practitioners' Association (ILPA) (2009) Response to a draft working document for statutory guidance under clause.57 of BIC Bill (now s.55 of the Borders, Citizenship and Immigration Act 2009) for comment 11 June 2009 Version 1.6 entitled *'Arrangements to Safeguard and Promote the Welfare of Children for those Exercising UK Border Agency functions and Director of Border Revenue functions'.* London: ILPA.

Joint Committee on Human Rights (2007) *The Treatment of Asylum Seekers: Tenth Report of Session 2006-7.* London: The Stationery Office. Accessed on 31 May 2011 at www.publications.parliament.uk/pa/jt200607/jtselect/jtrights/81/81i.pdf_

Kelly, E. (2009) *Bordering on Concern: Child Trafficking in Wales.* Swansea: Children's Commissioner for Wales and ECPAT UK.

Pearce, J., Hynes, P. and Bovarnick, S. (2009) *Breaking the Wall of Silence: Practitioners' Responses to Trafficked Children and Young People.* London: NSPCC.

R (B) v Merton London Borough Council [2003] EWHC 1689 (Admin), [2003] 4 All ER 280.

Refugee Council (2005) *Ringing the Changes: The Impact of Guidance on the Use of Sections 17 and 20 of the Children Act 1989 to Support Unaccompanied Asylum-Seeking Children.* London: Refugee Council.

Refugee Council (2007) *Determining the Duty to Look After Unaccompanied Children under the Children Act 1989 (use of section 17 or section 20).* Accessed on 31 May 2011 at www.refugeecouncil.org.uk/Resources/Refugee%20Council/downloads/briefings/wandsworthjudgment_briefing.pdf

Scottish Refugee Council (2009) *Improving the Lives of Children in Scotland – Are We There Yet? Consultation on the Scottish Government's Response to the 2008 Concluding Observations from the UN Committee on the Rights of the Child.* Glasgow: Scottish Refugee Council. Accessed on 20 Juy 2011 at www.scottishrefugeecouncil.org.uk/policy_and_research/information_and_resources/p29s1

Separated Children in Europe Programme (SCEP) (2010) *Statement of Good Practice: Separated Children in Europe Program,* 4th edn. Denmark: Save the Children.

Shaw, C., Brodie, I., Ellis, A., Graham, B. *et al.* (2010) *Research into Private Fostering.* London: DCSF.

United Kingdom Border Agency (UKBA) (2008) *UK Border Agency Code of Practice for Keeping Children Safe from Harm.* London: UKBA.

United Nations (1989) *Convention on the Rights of the Child.* New York: United Nations.

United Nations (2000) *Protocol to Prevent, Suppress, and Punish Trafficking in Persons, Especially Women and Children, Supplementing the United Nations Convention against Organized Crime.* New York: UN General Assembly.

United Nations High Commissioner for Refugees (UNHCR) (1997) *Guidelines on Policies and Procedures in Dealing with Unaccompanied Children Seeking Asylum.* Geneva: UNHCR.

Chapter Two

Identification of Separated Children in the UK

Philip Ishola

Introduction

In this chapter I discuss how we identify separated children and assess their individual needs, and how we identify, safeguard and protect child victims of trafficking. A range of specialist child trafficking identification and protection tools have been developed, including the child trafficking risk assessment indicator matrix, child trafficking assessment tool, child trafficking good practice guide and the child trafficking multi-agency strategic response guidance. I also describe how the *London Safeguarding Trafficked Children Toolkit* assisted in enhancing existing child trafficking good practice and developing the local, regional and national response to this issue (London SCB 2011c). This framework and guidance was piloted as the London SCB's *London Safeguarding Trafficked Children Toolkit* in 2009 in 12 local authority areas across the UK and monitored by a national monitoring group consisting of representatives of various interested stakeholders, which I chaired. I illustrate key points of practice through the exploration of two detailed case studies.

Rise in separated children

The global situation of heightened conflict and regional environmental disaster has since the mid-1990s led to a marked increase in the numbers of separated children. This phenomenon has led to a significant increase in the number of children who arrive in the UK as separated children and enter the asylum system, at which point they are deemed to be, for immigration purposes, unaccompanied asylum seeking children (UASC). Separated children claim asylum for a range of reasons, including flight from war, political conflict, and persecution on the basis of religion, ethnicity and faith. It is important to highlight that separated children may have a range of physical and mental health needs due to their experiences in their country of origin or on their journey to the UK.

The precise number of UASC in the UK is recorded by the Home Office and United Kingdom Border Agency (UKBA). However, it should be noted that the data capture only those children who have claimed asylum in the UK. The number of 'hidden children', those not known to any agency, is unknown; however, experience tells us there are a number of children separated from their family living in the UK with no support from statutory agencies.

The identification of separated children

Separated children enter the UK through various ports of entry (sea and air) and may or may not claim asylum at this point. Where a child arrives at a UK port unaccompanied, the UKBA would hold the child in the port holding suite while a referral is made to the local children's social care service. The child has the opportunity to claim asylum; if so, he or she will be classified as an UASC and referred to the local children's social care team. However, if the UKBA immigration officer believes the child may be older than he or she claims, that is an adult aged 18 years or over, the child may be held in an adult detention centre for a period of time while his or her age is determined via an age assessment, which would be carried out by qualified social workers. This can delay the identification process, because a request for an age assessment of an age disputed child in a detention centre may take time: it is reliant on a quick referral from UKBA to children's social care and a speedy response from children's social care, which is not always the case due, for example, to capacity issues within a social care team.

A separated child may sometimes be escorted through the UK border control point by an agent and be abandoned in the port (either before or after going through immigration) or during the journey from the port, for example on a motorway at a service station or in a town, placing the vulnerable child at risk of harm as he or she may be alone and may not speak English. Separated children may also enter the UK clandestinely in a cargo container, for example on a lorry or train, or in the boot of a car, and if they remain undetected, they may again leave the transport on a motorway at a service station or in a town. Children have been known to attempt to enter the UK under the carriages of trains and even aeroplanes, with tragic consequences. In 2002 the frozen bodies of two stowaways were discovered huddled together in the undercarriage of a passenger jet at

Heathrow Airport. The boys, who were aged between 12 and 14, stowed away on the six-hour flight from Accra in Ghana. The clandestine entry method is one of the key early events which forces a child into a position where the risk of harm is increased; it is without question an issue for agencies involved in identifying a child as separated and ensuring his or her safety. Where children enter the UK clandestinely, it is likely they would not know where to go or what to do to receive help. They may be reliant on the help of strangers, which will always increase the risk to their safety and may mean separated children are kept away from statutory agencies and possibly exploited. However, many entry routes and drop off points are known and monitored by the police, who spot these children, hold them and refer them to children's social care.

There are several way in which a separated child may arrive at a children's social care office, including referrals from UKBA, police, solicitor firms, non-governmental organisations (NGOs), faith and community groups, health professionals, adults presenting with a child or a child presenting on his or her own. In each case the child in need or child protection framework should define the immediate response depending on the unique circumstances of that child. Immigration and asylum issues, although important, should follow the provision of care and support for a child.

Where a separated child arrives and does not claim asylum at port, he or she will be referred to the local children's social care team, where as part of the child in need assessment framework social workers will assess the range of needs that a child may have (Department of Health 2000). The outcome of this assessment would (unless the child is assessed as an adult) lead to that child being accommodated under Section 20 of the Children Act 1989. The assessment of need process will include looking at the circumstances that led the child to flee his or her country of origin, which in turn may mean the child should claim asylum. However, it is not the role of children's social care to offer advice on immigration matters but to facilitate the child's access to specialist immigration legal advice. As part of the normal separated children's support package, children's social care would provide the child with access to good legal advice. So for social workers working with separated children, there are a number of additional tasks and considerations which extend the assessment process (and potentially add to the stress of the child). Another task is an age assessment, the outcome of which will determine if a child receives a service or not. Finally, the child will also have to repeat his or her story several times during the first few weeks and months after arrival, to solicitors, to the UKBA local immigration team (LIT), who determine all applications for asylum, and to children's social care.

Children's social care as the corporate parent is required to support the child through this process in addition to the statutory service provision as defined for all looked after children. Table 2.1 lists the assessment processes a separated child must navigate.

Table 2.1 Assessment processes for separated children

Children's social care assessment	Asylum assessment
Initial assessment	At port interview or at screening unit
Age assessment	Interview with solicitor
Core assessment	LIT screening interview
Looked after care review (every three months)	
Care Plan or Pathway Plan	

All separated children claiming asylum in the UK will have their application assessed and determined by a LIT case owner. All children who have been recognised as children following an age assessment (or where the child is clearly a child under the age of 14 where no age assessment is required) receive interim leave to remain in the UK up to the age of 17½ years. The young person, with support from their social worker, must then apply for further leave to remain in the UK. A separated child may receive a final determination at this point, which could be indefinite leave to remain, leave to remain under humanitarian protection or a negative determination (his or her application for asylum refused with an option to appeal). Or the child may not have received an outcome at all, pending the determination of his or her application for additional leave to remain in the UK. This is a critical time for separated children as the uncertainty of their future in the UK and the issues they may have experienced which led to their asylum claim come to the fore.

Detention centres

The detention of children is a thorny issue because the current UK government position is that no child should be detained for immigration purposes (asylum). However, there will be circumstances where a child may be in the asylum process but has committed a crime which a court has determined requires a custodial sentence or bail restrictions. The age dispute question and age assessment process play a crucial role in facilitating the detention of a child or enabling the child's release from detention to the care of children's social care respectively. For example, where an individual claims to be a child (who may be within the asylum process or who has yet to claim asylum) is detained because the authorities believe he or she may be an adult, the individual is likely to be held in an adult detention centre. The process to determine the age of the individual is critical. The outcome of the age assessment determines if the individual remains in detention or is recognised as a child and released into the care of a local authority, where the child's needs are assessed and the full range of care provision determined by the assessment is afforded to the child. There are inherent risks associated with this process for a child as an age assessment is entirely dependent on a referral from either UKBA or the detention centre where the child may be held. If the individual has not claimed asylum, has limited or no immigration documents, and no legal representation or access to immigration legal advice, it may mean that the assumptions made by those disputing the individual's age may lead to the individual's removal from the UK without any children's social care intervention.

A small number of children's services will, if contacted by the Home Office, UKBA or the police, carry out an age assessment in a detention centre even though the child is not necessarily entitled to a service from that local authority (not the local authority area in which the detention centre is located). This is done in the belief that the best interests of the child come first, which necessitates the speedy facilitation of an age assessment. If any safeguarding, child protection or mental or physical health needs are identified during this process, children's social care immediately bring into force the children's welfare framework so as to ensure that the needs of the child are met.

It should be noted that UK and EU guidance and law state that a child claiming to be a child should be afforded the benefit of the doubt until such time as his or her age can be determined; the detention of individuals claiming to be a child can in certain circumstances be at variance to this guidance and law. There will always be circumstances where an adult who is clearly an adult claims to be a child. The age assessment process is not in place to provide services to adults pending an age determination. Individuals awaiting the outcome of an age assessment or a disputed age determination can present a significant challenge to Children's social care in terms of placement. The age assessment process is not definitive and there are risks associated with placing individuals in a children's social care establishment or foster care who have been assessed as children but who later turn out to be adults.

As part of our analysis of the assessment of need, we ask children who have been held in detention to tell us about their experiences. The children have consistently said they felt frightened and did not understand what was happening and why. They did not understand why no one would believe their age (what they were saying) and did not trust anyone; they all missed their parents, siblings and family and some believed they would never be released (in UK professional terms they are traumatised). These feelings continued after their release. Hence the importance for all agencies working in whatever capacity with separated children to approach their work from a child-centred and separated child needs aware approach. It can make a great difference to the life chances of a separated child (see Case 2.1).

Case 2.1: Hung's experiences while migrating

This case study demonstrates the complex and often dangerous journey for a separated child – a not uncommon experience.

Hung, a boy of 15 or 16, arrived in the UK in the back of a lorry in 2004. Hung's journey had started three or possibly four months ago (Hung was unsure how long he was travelling): 'I stopped counting the days as I thought I would never get where I was going'. Hung started his journey by car, travelling for six days before arriving in a country he did not know, Hung had eaten only once every day – 'a little rice and meat'. When Hung arrived, he was housed with 18 other people, including families with small children. Hung remained at this property for five to six weeks and was not allowed out of the house for his entire stay. Hung, along with the others, were then moved to a forest, where they boarded a lorry and travelled for a further nine days. On arrival in a European county (Hung was unsure which country it was) the group set out on foot, walking for over a week. Hung said: 'I was ill and always hungry'. Hung was aware that the numbers of people in the group reduced as the days went on. He believed some of the younger children died on the walk. Hung was reluctant to talk about this experience further. Hung remained in a house which he believed to be in France for a further two weeks or so, then set out with a group of young adults and children with an agent for the coast.

Hung lived in a forest near the coast for a number of weeks before hiding in a lorry, which boarded a ferry and arrived in the UK several hours later. Hung remained on the lorry for several hours, alighting when it stopped at what transpired was a service station on the M1 motorway. Hung and one other child were detained walking along the motorway by the police. Hung claimed to be 14 and wanted to claim asylum, Hung was referred by the police to children's services. As Hung had indicated a wish to claim asylum, legal representation was arranged and an application made. In the meantime Hung was thought to be an adult and provided with temporary accommodation in a bed and breakfast hotel. Hung was advised to seek advice from a NGO. After four months the local authority looked again at his age; Hung was deemed likely to be a child and was provided with support under Section 17 of the Children Act 1989.

This case study highlights a number of areas where the needs of the child were not at the centre of the assessment. The immigration process was initially the defining process which delayed the 'child in need support' that Hung required. The case study also indicates the misuse of Section 17 to provide accommodation for a child.

The Hillingdon Judgment 2003 is a landmark judgment made regarding the use of Sections 17 and 20 of the Children Act 1989 to accommodate children. The Hillingdon Judgment determined that children should be 'looked after' by the local authority under Section 20 rather than use Section 17. This judgment in actuality required children's social care to provide a child-centred provision of service based on the needs of a child and in line with services provided to UK children. This approach has been termed by some as the Children First approach to separated children.

Child trafficking

There are no concrete data on the exact number of children trafficked to the UK. Following the UK government's ratification of the Council of Europe Convention on Action against Trafficking in Human Beings in December 2005, a National Referral Mechanism (NRM) was implemented for adults and children trafficked into and within the UK on 1 April 2009. The NRM set out to formalise the UK process for victim identification and referral to support, providing a multi-agency framework within which partners from all sectors can cooperate and facilitate their access to advice, accommodation and support. The purposes of the Convention as described in Article 1 are:

(a) to prevent and combat trafficking in human beings, while guaranteeing gender equality;

(b) to protect the human rights of the victims of trafficking, design a comprehensive framework for the protection and assistance of victims and witnesses, while guaranteeing gender equality, as well as to ensure effective investigation and prosecution;

(c) to promote international cooperation on action against trafficking in human beings.

The NRM is a framework for identifying victims of human trafficking and ensuring they receive the appropriate care. Authorised agencies, such as the police, UKBA, social services and certain NGOs, who encounter potential victims of human trafficking, can refer them to the 'competent authority'. The initial referrer is known as the 'first responder'. In the UK, the competent authorities are the UK Human Trafficking Centre (UKHTC) and the UKBA. The UKHTC deals with referrals from the police, local authorities and NGOs. The UKBA deals with referrals identified as part of the immigration process. UKHTC refers all cases where there is an asylum claim or where the child is from outside the EU (non-EEA national) to the UKBA as competent authority; the UKBA assesses if the child is or is not a victim of trafficking under the Council of Europe Convention on Action against Trafficking in Human Beings (2005).

Decision making

The referrals are sent to a central contact point using a standard referral form. The case is then allocated to the relevant competent authority for an initial decision based on whether there are reasonable grounds to believe the individual is a potential victim of human trafficking. The 'reasonable grounds' decision is based on the information supplied on the referral form. The competent authority aims to make this initial decision within five working days of receiving the referral. If the initial decision is positive, the child will be granted a recovery and reflection period of 45 days. The child's legal representative and first responder are both notified of the decision by letter. It was agreed shortly after the April 2009 implementation date that a child should not receive the decision letter directly, be it positive or negative, as this may add to the trauma of the victim. During the 45-day recovery and reflection period, the competent authority gathers further information relating to the referral from the first responder and multi-agency colleagues. This additional information is used to make a full and conclusive decision on whether the referred person is a victim of human trafficking. The competent authority aims to make the decision within the 45-day recovery and reflection period. The referred person and the first responder are both notified of the decision by letter. The reflection period for children is more relevant for children's social care, because it allows time to safeguard and protect a suspected victim and to carry out the multi-agency investigation. Practitioners have found that 45 days as a timeframe to obtain information from a child to support a referral via the NRM with a view to obtaining a positive decision is too short, because information may come to light or be disclosed by the child much later in the investigation, if at all. However, the 45-day reflection period can be extended.

The trafficking of children is substantively carried out by organised criminal gangs, although children are also trafficked by small groups of adults, families and single individuals (CEOP 2010). But from a child's perspective, who actually takes a lead role in the trafficking may be completely irrelevant as the experience of physical and physiological trauma, separation, loss and abuse remains the same. CEOP's research (2009, 2010) has been invaluable in assisting statutory childcare agencies, police and wider law enforcement agencies in developing trafficked children risk profiles, holistic victim identification tools and trafficked childcare plans designed to ensure the provision of need is provided based on the specific experience of trafficking victims. As an individual directly involved in developing and implementing the *London Safeguarding Trafficked Children Guidance and Toolkit* (London SCB 2011a) and Harrow Children's Services *Good Practice Guidance for Trafficked Children in Care* (Harrow Council 2011), I have become convinced that the development of at risk child profiles based on the type of exploiter is critical in aiding identification of victims, which then triggers the holistic assessment and care provision via an integrated multi-agency response. However, there is one important element that runs through the entire response to child victims, which is the voice of the child. As part of my work I have always taken the view that children are asked what it is that makes them 'feel safe'. What they say is incorporated into all aspects of their protection plan and from their wider disclosure incorporated back into enhancing the risk profiles and identification tools; this is a complex and extended process but an extremely important one. I have found through the implementation of these tools that the type of trafficker is important; for example, children trafficked by organised criminal gangs are more likely to be trafficked for sexual exploitation, criminal activity or labour exploitation, whereas children who are trafficked for domestic servitude are more likely to be trafficked by small groups of traffickers or families. The risk profiles assist in early identification, and early identification means that children are protected.

The UK child welfare legislative framework, the Children Act 1989, is designed to safeguard and protect all children; however, historically there have been difficulties in providing these services to trafficked victims. One specific difficulty relates to identifying separated children who arrive in the

UK through routes other than ports of entry. As detailed above, children's reliance on adults with no parental responsibly or family connection (loosely termed as agents), who may have arranged for these children to be smuggled through the UK border and traffickers for the purpose of openly exploiting children or clandestinely trafficking children to the UK, means that the children are particularly vulnerable. These children may not immediately be known to children's statutory agencies, which increases the risk of harm to them and delays the safeguarding process when they do become known. The asylum application process adds to an already complex process of identification of need and referral to relevant support services. Some separated children are identified by traffickers as soft targets and groomed for exploitation; in addition other child or adult victims who remain under the control of their trafficker are used to lure new young people in to exploitative situations. From the organised criminal gang's perspective, the risk that their criminal activity will be discovered is substantially reduced. So the risk to separated children is real and present, and the risk to all children is likely to increase as experience tells us an active criminal gang whose activities remain undetected are likely to become (given time) more sophisticated in their operations and confident enough to start widening their list of potential victims. I use some or all of the following terms every day in my work: awareness raising, identification, protection, prevention, prosecution, disruption, intelligence gathering, information sharing, and multi-agency and partnership working. I have seen every one of those terms being implemented as a single agency response to good effect, and in my experience the most important and effective term is 'multi-agency and partnership working', because this approach delivers the most effective method to protect child victims of trafficking in all circumstances (see Case 2.2).

Case 2.2: Tuan's experiences of being found in a cannabis factory

This case study demonstrates the complexities of identifying a child as trafficked and how a range of agencies working together to safeguard and protect the child victim enhances the process of protection. This case study also details the specific tools developed by local authorities and the London SCB prior to and during the pilot phase of the *London Safeguarding Trafficked Children Toolkit.*

Contact

Tuan became known to the local authority's Youth Offending Team (YOT) during his court trial where the YOT was in attendance. Tuan had been arrested when police entered a cannabis factory where he was working after neighbours had alerted the police of their concerns. A worker from YOT contacted the local children's services Unaccompanied Minors Team (UMT) to express their suspicions that Tuan might have been a victim of trafficking. The young person had disclosed during his court trial that he had been kidnapped from another area in the UK and brought to the local authority's area.

Trafficking referral to children's services

The UMT child trafficking lead social worker referenced the child trafficking multi-agency strategic response guidance and contacted all involved agencies and agencies that were likely to become involved (creating the virtual child trafficking contact group, this group would later meet as part of the normal strategic safeguarding child protection meeting framework). They initiated a child trafficking assessment using the Child Trafficking Assessment Tool. During the assessment process, Tuan disclosed he had been 'befriended' by people who he had met while sleeping rough in Kent. The people offered him accommodation and food. In return he was expected to work for them in cannabis factories looking after their plants. He was often moved around from house to house and was never introduced to anyone else. Tuan had been given a mobile that he could answer and make outgoing calls to his boss. Tuan was beaten if he refused to carry out any tasks. On one occasion when Tuan attempted to refuse to move house, the boss held his face over a gas cooker; this required hospital treatment. It was noted that one of Tuan's ears appeared deformed; the young person denied that this was due to any beatings that he had received. Tuan was guarded when discussing his experiences in his country of origin (trafficking profile) and route to the UK (movement).

Children's services initiate multi-agency response

On receiving the referral from the YOT, the UMT trafficking lead social worker contacted all involved agencies, including YOT, Crown Prosecution Service (CPS), the arresting police officers and health, detailing the process which was about to commence. The UMT then contacted the UKBA in order to establish if the child was known to the agency or had made an asylum claim; there was no record of the child. The UMT also ran a search through the National Register for Unaccompanied Children database (NRUC) and again no trace of Tuan was found.

Multi-agency trafficking response

Tuan was charged with the cultivation of cannabis and attended the local authority's youth court. Tuan was remanded at a Young Offenders Institute (YOI). As part of the multi-agency assessment process, the UMT either met with or obtained via the secure electronic information exchange process with the YOT, CPS, arresting police officers and the YOI information held by them in order to ensure all agencies contributed to the trafficking assessment process. All agencies were kept informed of any additional information arising from the assessment process which may require an agency-specific response. At this time it was not possible for bail to be granted as immigration had issued an IM3. An IM3 is a form used by UKBA to notify a claimant of their liability to deportation. (Any person of 17 years or over who does not have the right of abode and who is convicted of an offence for which he is liable to a custodial sentence may be recommended for deportation by a court which has the power to sentence him.) Tuan pleaded not guilty and re-presented at court four weeks later for a further bail/remand hearing, with his trial three weeks after this date. The UMT and YOT supported Tuan by being present during further court appearances. The UMT began a process to locate a specialist foster placement in the event that bail was granted or charges dropped. The trafficking assessment continued throughout the legal process, with regular visits to the YOI to assess and support Tuan.

Charges dropped and young person released into local authority care

The UMT completed the child trafficking assessment, the outcome of which confirmed Tuan as a victim of trafficking. The UMT submitted findings to the UK Human Trafficking Centre Competent Authority, using the NRM child referral form. They assessed the young person to have met the threshold criteria to be a trafficked child. Tuan was found to have reasonable and then conclusive grounds that confirmed this. The UMT findings were presented to the court. The court acknowledged that Tuan had been identified as a victim of trafficking and as a result the charges were dropped against Tuan (given that under international law child victims cannot consent to their own exploitation) and Tuan was released into the care of the local authority.

It is important to remember that the trafficking assessment provided a mechanism to obtain evidence which enabled the clear determination that Tuan was indeed a victim of child trafficking. However, child trafficking sits within the normal safeguarding and child protection legislative framework. The specific needs of children based on their experiences including the specific safeguards for trafficked children should continue using the existing local and national assessment frame as for any child in need.

The way forward

Having chaired the London SCB child safeguarding group, pilot group and monitoring group over three years, I have been able to look in detail at the difficulties that all statutory agencies face when trying to identifying child victims of trafficking. We created the London Trafficked Children Initiative to assist with this. In the context of the UK government's ratification of the Council of Europe Convention on Action against Trafficking in Human Beings in December 2005 and its implementation from 1 April 2009, the London SCB launched the London Trafficked Children Initiative in January 2008. This 18-month project has three main aims:

- Developing and sharing good practice in local safeguarding responses to trafficked children for local safeguarding children boards and their partner agencies.

- Assisting the integration of national trafficked children mechanisms with existing safeguarding children procedure and practice.

- Contributing to the redrafting of the 2006 London Child Protection Committee Safeguarding Trafficked Children Guidance incorporating learning from the 2009/10 pilot project.

In pursuit of these aims, the London SCB developed the *London Safeguarding Trafficked Children Toolkit* to provide guidance and tools for local multi-agency responses to trafficked children. From January 2009 to May 2010 12 local authorities across the UK agreed to pilot the toolkit: the pilot authorities were Camden, Croydon, Glasgow, Harrow, Hillingdon, Hounslow, Islington, Kent, Manchester, Slough, Solihull and Southwark. In March 2010 the pilot phase was completed. The tools developed for the pilot have now been evaluated and have proved invaluable to statutory agencies, who are endeavouring to identify, safeguard and protect child victims of trafficking.

Key findings

Overall, the *London Safeguarding Trafficked Children Toolkit* has helped pilot authorities to develop, implement and strengthen good practice in the safeguarding of trafficked children. Certain tools and sections of the guidance were widely used in this identification. However, rather than just being a set of discrete tools, the toolkit offered pilot authorities a comprehensive framework with which to approach the safeguarding of trafficked children. At the heart of this framework is multi-agency working, which recognises that trafficking is a complex form of child abuse and requires a proactive response supported by specialist training and input from professionals, voluntary groups and community agencies alike. These factors include strong leadership, staff specialism, robust identification and assessment processes, multilevel interagency training and consistent, informed multi-agency engagement throughout the safeguarding process.

Such factors and others are captured in the following six key findings, which particularly address the persistent challenges faced by pilot authorities in developing and maintaining a multi-agency approach. First, identification of trafficked children is a major challenge for pilot local authorities in a context of low public awareness, professional reluctance to accept child trafficking as a live issue in the UK, inconsistent levels of multi-agency engagement, and the rapid speed with which trafficked children can go missing. Second, some trafficked children face strong pressure to go missing, that is to return to the trafficker or trafficking network, within 24 hours of being identified. All agencies need to recognise the challenges faced in safeguarding these children and the importance of the first 'golden hour' in rapidly implementing safeguarding measures for newly identified trafficked children. Third, many authorities compare trafficking to other child protection issues such as child sexual abuse, where extensive training and awareness building is needed across all agencies and the general public to build acceptance of the issue as child abuse and to develop skills to respond to it. Child trafficking needs to be recognised as a highly complex area of child protection that requires an intensive, concerted and *resourced* response. Fourth, pilot authorities rated the risk assessment matrix for children who may have been trafficked (in the London SCB (2001c) *Safeguarding Trafficked Children Toolkit*) as the most useful tool, considered a 'must-have' by two-thirds of them, though it may be problematic for younger children (see Figure 2.1). A concern exists where the risk assessment matrix is being used in place of the trafficking assessment – a shorter version of the trafficking assessment is likely to be used more widely. Fifth, the assessment of children suspected of being trafficked can be problematic. Short assessment timescales do not recognise the complexities of disclosure, and can reduce the quality of the trafficking assessment and traumatise children. Additional information often emerges after initial investigations, and practitioners find it difficult to change initial assessments and lack clarity on how to input newly disclosed information on trafficking following NRM decisions. In addition, multiple interviews by various agencies can be traumatic for a child; more streamlined information-gathering through a single, holistic, multi-agency interview is preferred. Finally, age assessments remain a controversial issue for child protection and asylum teams. Pilot authorities felt strongly that decisions about the age of trafficked children are best made through social interaction and social work assessment.

Identification and assessment

An innovation to note is that some local authorities are using the toolkit in conjunction with the CEOP strategic threat assessment to help identify trafficked children. Two councils use information from both sources as well as local statistics to profile and identify children at risk of going missing and/or being trafficked. They then implement the *Good Practice Guidance for Trafficked Children in Care* (Harrow Council 2011) to reduce this risk. One local authority undertakes the trafficking assessment only after implementing good practice measures to reduce the risk of a child going missing. Since using the good practice guide, the authority no longer places children at risk of being trafficked in shared homes (London SCB 2011a, p.19). The introduction of a lead child trafficking safeguarding coordinator in the children's services department of each local authority could greatly assist identification of trafficked children, as the coordinator could coordinate the safeguarding response using a multi-agency approach. Other measures to improve identification include recognising that training and/or awareness-raising is critical in building local authority and multi-agency safeguarding capacity. All pilot authorities provided some degree of training to a broad range of teams, the police and the voluntary and community sector. However, more training is needed, particularly of frontline and first responder services. This training needs to reflect the multi-agency response required to address child trafficking, with a wide selection of agencies involved in training and/or the identification and assessment process. Trafficked children are safeguarded best where a multi-agency approach is working well. However, it takes considerable time to build a level playing field in local authority capacity to deal with trafficking and to develop effective multi-agency working. The UKBA is recognised by local authorities as a new partner around the child protection table.

Child development

Exploitation	Y	S
Claims to have been exploited through sexual exploitation, criminality, labour exploitation, domestic servitude, forced marriage, illegal adoption, and drug dealing by another person.		
Physical symptoms of exploitative abuse (sexual, physical etc)		
Underage marriage		
Physical indications of working (overtly tired in school, indications of manual labour – condition of hands/skin, backaches etc)		
Sexually transmitted infection or unwanted pregnancy		
Story very similar to those given by others, perhaps hinting they have been coached		
Significantly older boyfriend		
Movement in / within UK	**Y**	**S**
Returning after missing, looking well cared for despite no base		
Claims to have been in the UK for years but hasn't learnt local language or culture		
Other risk factors	**Y**	**S**
Withdrawn and refuses to talk / appears afraid to talk to a person in authority		
Harbours excessive fears / anxieties (e.g. about an individual, of deportation, disclosing information etc)		
Shows signs of physical neglect – basic care, malnourishment, lack of attention to health needs		
Shows signs of emotional neglect		
Socially isolated – lack of positive, meaningful relationships in child's life		
Behavioural - poor concentration or memory, irritable / unsociable / aggressive behaviour in school or placement		
Psychological – indications of trauma or numbing		
Exhibits self assurance, maturity and self confidence not expected in a child of such age		
Evidence of drug, alcohol or substance misuse		
Low self image, low self esteem, self harming behaviour including cutting, overdosing, eating disorder, promiscuity		
Sexually active		
Not registered with or attended a GP practice		
Not enrolled in school		
Has money, expensive clothes, mobile phones or other possessions without plausible explanation		

Parenting capacity

Exploitation	Y	S
Required to earn a minimum amount of money every day		
Involved in criminality highlighting involvement of adults (e.g. recovered from cannabis farm / factory, street crime, petty theft, pick pocketing, begging etc)		
Performs excessive housework chores and rarely leaves the residence		
Reports from reliable sources suggest likelihood of sexual exploitation, including being seen in places known to be used for sexual exploitation		
Unusual hours / regular patterns of child leaving or returning to placement which indicates probable working		
Accompanied by an adult who may not be the legal guardian and insists on remaining with the child at all times		
Limited freedom of movement		
Movement into / or within the UK	**Y**	**S**
Gone missing from local authority care		
Unable to confirm name or address of person meeting them on arrival		
Accompanying adult previously made multiple visa applications for other children / acted as the guarantor for other children's visa applications		
Accompanying adult known to have acted as guarantor on visa applications for other visitors who have not returned to their countries of origin on visa expiry		
History with missing links or unexplained moves		
Pattern of street homelessness		
Other risk factors	**Y**	**S**
Unregistered private fostering arrangement		
Cared for by adult/s who are not their parents and quality of relationship is not good		
Placement breakdown		
Persistently missing, staying out overnight or returning late with no plausible explanation		
Truancy / disengagement with education		
Appropriate adult is not an immediate family member (parent / sibling)		
Appropriate adult cannot provide photographic ID for the child		

Family / environment

Exploitation	Y	S
Located / recovered from a place of exploitation (brothel, cannabis farm, involved in criminality etc)		
Deprived of earnings by another person		
Claims to be in debt bondage or "owes" money to other persons (e.g. for travel costs, before having control over own earnings)		
Receives unexplained / unidentified phone calls whilst in placement / temporary accommodation		
No passport or other means of identity		
Unable or reluctant to give accommodation or other personal details		
False documentation or genuine documentation that has been altered or fraudulently obtained; or the child claims that their details (name, DOB) on the documentation are incorrect		
Movement into or within the UK	**Y**	**S**
Entered country illegally		
Journey or visa arranged by someone other than themselves or their family		
Registered at multiple addresses		
Other risk factors	**Y**	**S**
Possible inappropriate use of the internet and forming online relationships, particularly with adults		
Accounts of social activities with no plausible explanation of the source of necessary funding		
Entering or leaving vehicles driven by unknown adults		
Adults loitering outside the child's usual place of residence		
Leaving home / care setting in clothing unusual for the individual child (inappropriate for age, borrowing clothing from older people etc)		
Works in various locations		
One among a number of unrelated children found at one address		
Having keys to premises other than those known about		
Going missing and being found in areas where they have no known links		

Figure 2.1: Risk assessment matrix for children who may have been trafficked

Note: Shading indicates the need for an immediate referral to children's services as it indicates that a child is at risk of harm.

Police engagement with children's services on suspected trafficking cases is considered variable across boroughs: police can be reluctant to act on suspicions, even where the matrix is used. The degree of investigation that should be undertaken by social workers needs to be spelled out more clearly, especially where police involvement is limited or absent. Engagement is assisted by early identification of the borough's police trafficking lead, for example, the Public Protection Desk or Child Abuse Investigation Team and development of joint protocols. The voluntary and community sector has a useful role in providing specialist training and aiding the identification, assessment and recovery of trafficked young people; also their involvement in trafficking subgroups strengthens links into the community and helps build public awareness of trafficking.

Pilot authorities had a low-to-moderate level of awareness of the NRM but felt it had 'put trafficking on the map' locally and nationally; 47 cases of suspected child trafficking were referred by eight pilot authorities. There are difficulties, however, with the NRM timescales. Effective information-sharing is critical but can take a longer time than may be available to accurately assess and refer a child within the timeframes provided by the NRM, for example, the 45-day reflection period. Local authorities would prefer full engagement by all agencies during the case conference process and before a NRM referral is made, and by the competent authority after the NRM referral during the period know as the 'reasonable and conclusive grounds decision making'. Other learning indicates that local authorities require much more support from other agencies when undertaking their first few NRM referrals. Clarity is needed on when the referral should occur and how much information to provide. Pre-referral multi-agency meetings and a shared multi-agency decision *at the point of referral* was found to be very useful.

The future arrangements for trafficked children have improved since 2009 and in my view further considerable effort is still required in order to protect some of the most vulnerable children in this world. This can be achieved only through the closest partnership working arrangement between all agencies.

References

Child Exploitation and Online Protection Centre (CEOP) 2009 *Strategic Threat Assessment: Child Trafficking in the UK*. London. CEOP.

Child Exploitation and Online Protection Centre (CEOP) (2010) *Strategic Threat Assessment: Child Trafficking in the UK*. London: CEOP.

Council of Europe (2005) *Convention on Action against Trafficking in Human Beings*. Warsaw: COE.

Department of Health (2000) *Framework of Assessment of Need of Children and Their Families.* London: The Stationery Office.

Harrow Council (2011) *Good Practice Guidance for Trafficked Children in Care, Guidance Designed to Aid Social Care and Education Professionals, Foster Carers and Residential Staff to Meet to the Needs of Trafficked Children in Care.* London: Harrow Council.

London SCB (2011a) *Final Monitoring Report Local Authority Pilots of the London Safeguarding Trafficked Children Guidance and Toolkit.* London: London SCB.

London SCB (2011b) *London Safeguarding Trafficked Children Guidance.* London: London SCB.

London SCB (2011c) *London Safeguarding Trafficked Children Toolkit.* London: London SCB.

Chapter Three

Asylum, Age Disputes and the Process of Age Assessment

Heaven Crawley and Emma Kelly

Introduction

The determination of age is a difficult and often inexact task in which physical, social and cultural factors play a part. Many separated asylum seeking children experience significant difficulties in relation to the process and outcomes of an age assessment, with implications not only for their health and well-being but also for their ability to gain access to protection under international refugee law. Figures suggest that age disputed applicants are on the rise (Bhabha and Finch 2006; Crawley 2007), a view supported by the Joint Committee on Human Rights, which noted that 'in 2005 nearly half (45%) of all applications made by those presenting as unaccompanied asylum seeking children [UASC] were age disputed and the applicants treated as adults' (Joint Committee on Human Rights 2007, p.65).

Although the process of age assessment should be a holistic one, taking into account a range of social, emotional and psychological indicators of age and need, there is evidence of an over-reliance on physical characteristics and attributes (Crawley 2007). This problem is exacerbated by a lack of statutory guidance for local authorities with responsibility for the assessment of age, resulting in increasing and ongoing litigation in order to determine best practice. This chapter focuses on the circumstances under which the age of separated asylum seeking children is disputed and the process of age assessment undertaken by the children's services department of local authorities. It is suggested that continued doubt about the authenticity of separated asylum seeking children's statements in relation to their age stands in stark contrast to the accepted idea in safeguarding about 'how fundamentally important it is for a child to feel they are believed' (Nandy 2007, p.4). The chapter draws on in-depth research undertaken by the Immigration Law Practitioners' Association (ILPA) to explore the policy and practice of age disputes and assessment with United Kingdom Border Agency (UKBA), social workers and separated children (Crawley 2007).[1]

Why is age disputed?

Age assessments take place for a variety of reasons but underpinning them is bureaucratic doubt regarding the stated age of a separated child or young person. According to the joint protocol between the Association of Directors of Social Services (ADSS) and the UKBA in 2004, separated children who claim asylum may require an age assessment for two main reasons: first, UKBA needs to be clear about whether an applicant is over or under 18 because this will determine which asylum process and asylum support arrangements are appropriate; and second, the local authority has a statutory duty to assess the situation of children in need. In order to do so it may need to decide on an applicant's age. This applies not only to whether someone is aged 18 or over but also in relation to whether a child has reached the age of 16 as this affects rights to statutory education, as well as working and benefit entitlement.

An emphasis on age which is directly linked to eligibility for services is problematic because many separated children genuinely do not know their chronological age or date of birth. Not all countries and cultures attach the same importance to chronological age, and birth records may therefore be afforded less importance. In many countries birthdays are not marked. This may reflect the social and cultural context from which children originate, or conditions of poverty and/or conflict which render such celebrations impossible or inappropriate. When asked how old they are, many children calculate or guess their age on the basis of events that have happened in their lives or information that has been given to them by others prior to their departure (Crawley 2007). Children may also have grown up in economic and political contexts where being a child does not confer any particular rights or privileges, or indeed may be a distinct disadvantage in the fight for resources or even survival. These children are forced to grow up very quickly because there is no advantage to be gained from remaining 'childlike' or dependent for longer than absolutely necessary. Other complicating factors relating to age include cultural differences in

---

1   The findings of the ILPA research were published in a report entitled *When is a Child Not a Child? Asylum, Age Disputes and the Process of Age Assessment* (Crawley 2007). The report was launched at the Houses of Parliament in 2007 and resulted in a Home Office working group, which was established to explore ways in which current procedures for age assessment might be improved. The full report can be downloaded at www.ilpa.org. uk/publications/ILPA%20Age%20Dispute%20Report.pdf

talking about how old you are. For instance, in Iran, children are in their first year immediately after they are born. Differences in the significance given to chronological age and in the recording conventions and calendars of the countries and cultures from which many separated asylum seeking children originate can also create difficulties during the screening process.

Reflecting the contexts from which separated asylum seeking children originate, many are unable to present the documentary evidence of their age required by UKBA – an original and genuine passport, travel document, national identity card, or an original and genuine birth certificate (Home Office, undated). There is evidence that issues relating to documentation including birth certificates and identity cards can be a significant factor in the decision to dispute age and that this can be exacerbated by the use of different calendars in some countries of origin as noted above (Crawley 2007). Issues of documentation may also be tied in with the perceived credibility (or otherwise) of the child's account of his or her stated age and experiences. For example, where forged documents are produced, this may be perceived by the UKBA case owner, social worker or immigration judge as undermining the veracity of the account regardless of its content. Credibility assumes central importance in claims for asylum so perceived discrepancies in accounts from children can lead them to being completely disbelieved (Bhabha and Finch 2006; Crawley 2010, 2011).

Just as importantly, there is a belief on the part of the Home Office, which is shared by some social workers, that adults entering the UK deliberately claim to be children when seeking asylum in order to benefit from the advantages that this confers. Indeed, the Home Office's (2002) White Paper addressed the 'need to identify children in genuine need at the earliest possible stage, to sift out adults posing as children and to deter those seeking to abuse the system' (Home Office 2002, para. 4.55). Separated asylum seeking children will generally not be detained or subject to the fast-track procedures, and those whose asylum claims are refused are removed from the UK only if adequate care and reception arrangements are in place in their country of origin. In addition, separated children benefit from being looked after by local authorities under the Children Act 1989 in a context where access to welfare benefits is increasingly restrictive for adult asylum seekers. There is also a view that adults claim to be children in order to benefit from a period of discretionary leave until they are 17½ years of age.

The process of age assessment

The assessment of chronological age is notoriously difficult. Even among children who grow up in the same social and economic environment and come from similar ethnic backgrounds, there are significant physical and emotional differences, as well as differences in needs and vulnerability, between children of the same age. Separated asylum seeking children come from cultures and contexts in which childhood is defined in different ways and where the social, economic and political circumstances in which they live make it impossible for them to do the things that we expect children living in the UK to be able to do. Recognising these difficulties, international law stipulates upholding a child's best interests when making critical decisions about age. For example, the Council of Europe Trafficking Convention states that 'When the age of the victim is uncertain and there are reasons to believe that the victim is a child, he or she shall be presumed to be a child and shall be accorded special protection measures pending verification of his/her age' (Council of Europe 2005, Article 10(3)).

Despite this, there continues to be a strong interest in identifying a method of assessment which is able to provide an accurate indication of chronological age. Increasingly the emphasis has been placed on identifying medical 'tests' which can be used to assess age and which can reduce the perceived subjectivity of other forms of assessment. This is despite the fact that there is no reliable medical or other scientific test to establish chronological age (Crawley 2007). Although numerous medical tests exist, including the assessment of bone age, dental age assessments and the assessment of physical development (including puberty, height, weight, skin and bone), they all have a significant margin of error. This means that a paediatrician can conclude that a child is 16 but must acknowledge the potential for a margin of error of a minimum of two years, so in fact the young person could be between 14 and 18. The assessment of bone age and dental age is most commonly based on X-rays, but neither is recommended for non-medical purposes because of the dangers associated with unnecessary exposure to irradiation. The Royal College of Paediatrics and Child Health conclude: 'it is inappropriate for X-rays to be used merely to assist in age determination for immigration purposes' (RCPCH 2003, p.1). In addition, both bone age and dental age tests have a problematic research basis. Bone age tests are based primarily on research with Caucasian children and it is acknowledged that the margin of error increases with the age of the child. Dental tests results are described by the Royal College of Radiologists (2007) as 'variable'.

UKBA policy and practice

Although not all age disputes occur immediately on arrival, there is evidence to suggest that most age disputes arise when an individual first applies for asylum in the UK (Crawley 2007). The key concern in the early stages of the asylum process is that much of what currently passes for 'age assessment' undertaken by UKBA case owners at screening units and ports is essentially a rapid visual assessment based on physical appearance and demeanour. This assessment may conclude that an individual *doesn't look like a child* based on a socially constructed understanding of what a child should look like (Crawley 2007, 2010, 2011). Where the applicant's physical appearance or demeanour 'very strongly suggests that an individual is significantly over 18 years of age' (UKBA undated, p.4), he or she will be treated as an adult by UKBA and will fall within the adult process. Under these circumstances an individual will not be formally age assessed at the beginning of the asylum process, although in practice he or she may be assessed at a later date, for example, if an agency with whom an individual comes into contact is concerned that he or she may in fact be a child and that his or her health and welfare is potentially at risk, or if there are child protection concerns. For children who are determined by UKBA as being adults at this stage the consequences are potentially devastating. When a child enters the adult process, both the child and the paperwork associated with his or her case are moved physically to the adult section of the screening unit, and is required to wait his or her turn with other adults in what may be a very lengthy queue. Other reports indicate children being kept for long periods of time without basic necessities (including food and water) and not understanding what is happening to them (CCE 2008; Crawley 2007). These children do not benefit from any of the procedures that the Home Office has put in place to ensure that children's experiences and vulnerability are taken into account during the asylum determination process. The application may be refused and the individual detained and removed without ever having his or her age formally assessed. There is evidence that age disputed applicants are likely to be considered less credible and refused asylum as a result of being age disputed.

Disputes over age also have significant implications for the ability of children to access appropriate social welfare, health and educational support. In addition to the very significant practical consequences and child protection risks of being age disputed, there is evidence of significant mental health difficulties associated with the fact that a child's past and identity are brought into question (Crawley 2007). Many separated young people talk about the impact of not being believed. For Hakim (see Case 3.1) it led to frustration with children's services. Hakim's age assessment placed him at 16, rather than his true age of 13, which meant that he was also unable to go to school.

Case 3.1: Hakim's experience of multiple assessments

Hakim arrived in the UK in September 2005 after travelling for eight days in the back of a lorry from Turkey. He was picked up by the police in Dover and taken to the police station, where he was kept overnight in a cell. The next day he was interviewed by the Immigration Service and his age (13 years) was disputed. He was taken to Dover Immigration Removal Centre, but staff at the centre refused to accept him because they believed he was a child. He was returned to bed-and-breakfast (B&B) accommodation in Dover and then dispersed by the National Asylum Support Service (NASS) to a city in the midlands, where he lived in a house with another man, who tried to look after him as best he could.

During this time Hakim came into contact with an adviser from the Children's Panel, who referred him to social services for an age assessment. He was also assessed by a paediatrician. The social service age assessment process concluded that Hakim was 16 and he was placed with a foster family. Unfortunately the placement was not successful; Hakim ran away and returned to his NASS accommodation. The man he shared the accommodation with took him back to the social services department, which again placed him in a B&B. Hakim was upset and frustrated about the social services' assessment, which had concluded that he was 16 years of age. Later on social services readjusted this assessment on the basis of a birth certificate sent by Hakim's brother, who is living in Pakistan. Hakim is now living with a foster family and is in full-time education.

Where there are doubts about an individual's stated age but the individual is not considered by UKBA as being 'significantly over 18 years of age', he or she will be processed in the first instance as though a child but will be considered 'age disputed' and will be referred to the appropriate local authority for a formal assessment. As part of its duties, the local authority will normally conduct an assessment of the claimant's age in order to determine eligibility to children's services, and in some cases, the level of the person's needs (since the level of need may depend on age). This process raises important issues about the ways in which children's experiences are interpreted and how their needs are assessed.

Local authority practice

A separated asylum seeking child's stated age may be disputed by children's services as a result of a formal or informal process of age assessment. The dispute may reflect or confirm the Home Office's initial decision to dispute age or may arise as a result of an assessment of the young person's needs. In some cases children's services may decide to dispute a child's age even though the applicant has not been age disputed by the Home Office and is being treated as a separated child for the purpose of the asylum process. Alternatively the local authority may accept that the applicant is a child but may conclude that he or she is older than is claimed (Crawley 2007). It is important to note here that disputes over age are not only associated with whether or not someone is under 18 years of age: 16 years of age is also an important cut off point because it has significant implications for the level and type of care and accommodation provision to which a child or young person is entitled under the Children Act 1989, as illustrated in Case 3.1. This can lead to uncertainty and change in the early weeks of a young person's support in the UK as documented in recent research: 'Four of the children were confused and frightened by what was happening to them when they first arrived. They were moved between adult accommodation centres and hostels, supported accommodation and reception centres, and foster placements during their initial few weeks in England' (Brownlees and Finch 2010, p.45).

In theory, local authorities will assess age as part of the overall assessment of children in need rather than as a discrete process (IND and ADSS 2004). In practice, however, given that an age assessment often occurs before a needs assessment, the opportunities to safeguard children and promote their welfare at this stage are limited. Children's services may come into contact with young people in need of an age assessment in a variety of ways. First, they may receive referrals direct from UKBA, when a separated child has turned up at a port. Second, social workers based at the asylum screening units in Croydon and Liverpool can undertake an age assessment when a young person claims asylum. This assessment is most usually undertaken on the same day as the screening interview and can lead to confusion as to the purpose of the assessment and the role of the social worker. As the former Children's Commissioner for England has suggested:

> it is hard to see how a child or young applicant would be able to identify this local authority assessment as being anything other than a component of the screening process which, for all intents and purposes, it is...conducting an age assessment for this purpose, but at the request and within time scales designed

to meet the administrative needs of the BIA [UKBA], may lead
to a conflict of interest. (CCE 2008, p.16)

Third, some local authorities come into contact with age disputed young
people because they have been 'dispersed' as adults and are living in NASS
accommodation within their local authority area. Finally, some young
people are identified as children only once they have been placed in
detention centres, for example where a legal representative requests that a
formal age assessment be undertaken.

There is evidence of wide variation in whether or not an age assessment
is undertaken, even where a child whose age is disputed is referred to
children's services. Some local authorities do not routinely undertake
formal age assessments when they get referrals or come into contact with
children whose age is disputed. Conversely other separated children may
be age assessed on a number of separate occasions by a number of different
local authorities or they may be reassessed by the same local authority
sometimes with conflicting and contradictory results. The reasons for this
vary, but it is usually because new information has come to light (Crawley
2007). The experiences of Desta in Case 3.2 illustrate the impact of multiple
assessments on a young person and the length of time it can take for these
to be resolved. For separated children, like any other child, time is critical
and decision making should be timely; this principle is embedded in the
Separated Children in Europe Programme that 'all decisions regarding
separated children must be taken in a timely fashion taking into account the
child's perception of time. While all decisions should be given thorough
consideration, delay shall be presumed to be prejudicial to the child' (SCEP
2010, p.12).

Case 3.2: Desta's experiences of not being believed

Desta was 16 years old when she arrived in the UK and claimed
asylum at the airport. Her age was disputed, so she was placed in hostel
accommodation and referred to social services for an age assessment.
The age assessment interview was undertaken six weeks later with
the use of an Amharic interpreter. The social worker conducting
the interview considered that Desta answered his questions with
very little emotion, seemed to be withholding information and was
evasive. Her mannerisms were considered to be older than those of a
16-year-old. The social worker also asked a wide range of questions
about the basis of the asylum application and concluded that she was
avoiding some of his questions and that her account was inconsistent.
The social worker identified contradictions in the account given to

the paediatrician as further evidence that Desta was older than she claimed to be. He concluded that her desire to live on her own was demonstrative of the fact that she was older than she claimed to be.

Following the age assessment by social services, Desta stayed in a hostel in London for around a year before being dispersed to a city in the northeast of England. During this time her appeal against the refusal to grant asylum was dismissed. She was subsequently reassessed by the local social services in the area to which she was moved and accepted as being a child. She is currently being supported by them pending the conclusion of her case.

There is currently no statutory guidance on the process by which social workers should assess the age of separated asylum seeking children. In the absence of such guidance, the protocol which has been negotiated between the Home Office and ADSS sets out the process by which an age assessment will be undertaken (IND and ADSS 2006). It states that where UKBA (previously IND) is the first agency to come into contact with a child or young person, and doubts his or her stated age, the young person will be treated as an adult but may approach a local authority for a formal assessment of age. Where the local authority is the first point of contact, an age assessment should be conducted, ideally on the same day, and the outcome of that assessment relayed to UKBA. Throughout the ADSS protocol reference is made to a 'central point of contact' between social services departments and the UKBA through which information about the assessment process and its outcome should be relayed. The protocol also sets out the procedures which should be followed where there are conflicting assessments between the local authority and UKBA, or between local authorities.

The current approach for undertaking assessments of age has evolved through practice by social service departments and a growing number of legal challenges to local authority decisions. Since 2003 children's services have been required to undertake a 'Merton-compliant' age assessment following the findings of Burnton, J in R (B) v Merton London Borough Council [2003] EWHC. The guidance from the judgment has been the benchmark of best practice in age assessments since, all age assessments should follow the guidelines set out to ensure that they are compliant. According to the Children's Legal Centre (2003), the guidance stipulates the following:

- Age must not be determined solely on the basis of appearance.

- Assessment should cover general background, including family circumstances and history, educational background, and activities during the previous few years. Ethnic and cultural information will also be important.

- Physical appearance and behaviour cannot be isolated from the question of the veracity of the applicant: appearance, behaviour and the credibility of his or her account are all matters that reflect on each other (para. 28).

- If there is a reason to doubt the applicant's statement as to his or her age, the decision maker will have to make an assessment of the applicant's credibility, and will have to ask questions designed to test credibility (para. 37).

- Two workers should undertake the assessment and it should take place over a period of time and involve other professionals, such as residential social work staff, teachers, and other young people where appropriate.

- The assessment of age in borderline cases is a difficult matter, but it is not complex and can be determined informally, provided that safeguards of minimum standards of inquiry and of fairness are adhered to (para. 36).

- The social worker should ensure that the young person understands the role of the assessing worker and the interpreter.

In summary the assessment of age should be holistic and include the physical appearance and demeanour, the interaction of the person during assessment, social history and family composition, developmental compositions, education, independent and self-care skills, health and medical assessment, and information from documentation and other sources. It is worth mentioning the varying levels of expertise in undertaking an age assessment: in some areas there are dedicated teams working with separated asylum seeking children, but in local authority areas where there are very few separated children, age assessments are likely to be carried out by duty social workers who may have little experience or knowledge of the process (Crawley 2007; Kelly 2009).

The Merton Judgment has had both positive and negative implications for the process of age assessment. On the one hand, the Merton Judgment clearly states that age cannot be determined solely on the basis of physical appearance and that a wide range of different background factors should be taken into account. Assumptions should not be made in advance of the assessment process about whether the applicant is an adult or a child. The decision reached by the Home Office cannot simply be adopted by the local authority, but rather reasons for the outcome must be given. On the other hand, there is evidence that the Merton Judgment, and in particular the wording of the judge's conclusions in paragraph 37, has encouraged some local authorities to focus disproportionately on the credibility of an asylum seeker's account.

Despite the Merton Judgment, there continue to be inconsistencies in the use and interpretation of documentary, expert and medical evidence in the age assessment process (Crawley 2007). Although the age assessment process undertaken by local authorities is likely to be more comprehensive than the rapid visual assessment undertaken by immigration officers at the screening units and ports, there is currently an over-reliance on social service age assessments, which are often not very good. Judicial reviews of the process by which age is assessed have also raised questions about the assessment process itself and, specifically, about the weight that should be given to evidence provided by experts such as paediatricians and whether immigration tribunals can make decisions about age. In R (NA) v Croydon [2009] EWCH 2357, the authenticity of documents and demeanour were central features of the case. In this case the social workers questioned the authenticity of a 15-year-old's birth certificate and concluded that he was in fact 17, a decision which they supported by suggesting that his demeanour was of a young person of that age (even though he physically looked younger). In R (PM) v Hertfordshire County Council [2010] EWHC 2056, the local authority accepted the opinion of an immigration tribunal judge that the claimant was over 18. It was found on appeal that it is the responsibility of the local authority to conduct an age assessment: '[it is the council] who must exercise their own judgment in assessing the Claimant's age for the purposes of their section 20 duty [under the Children Act 1989]' (para. 83).

The future of age assessments

The future of age assessments remains unclear. What is clear is that the current process continues to be deeply problematic for UKBA case owners, social workers and children and young people themselves, many of whom find themselves locked into a complex and time-consuming process of litigation in order to secure access to the protection and services to which they are entitled. Children and young people who are age disputed and are either not assessed at all or incorrectly assessed as adults have a right to contest the assessment, but this is currently possible only with the assistance of a legal representative and usually requires new evidence to be produced in relation to the applicant's claimed age. This new evidence is usually medical evidence, although on occasions other documentation is identified. Throughout the process of a legal dispute over age, the treatment that a young person receives will depend on the approach by the local authority involved in the case. Some local authorities will give children and young people the benefit of the doubt and offer them support while the age dispute is resolved. Others will treat the applicant as an adult unless and until the courts judge that he or she must be treated as a child. This can mean being placed in inappropriate accommodation or without necessary support and education for the duration of the dispute. In some cases, disputes over age and over the process of age assessment can continue over several years, during which time the separated child is effectively in limbo. More distressing still is the fact that removal directions can, and sometimes do, arrive, even though removal is not possible because the matter is before the courts.

It is in the interests of all concerned, and particularly for the children and young people seeking asylum, that a mechanism is established for independently reviewing the *process* by which the conclusion about an individual's age has been reached *before* recourse to the courts. There is evidence that ongoing disputes over age can become focused on small and seemingly insignificant issues or events which gain significance as the legal process proceeds. This problem appears to be closely associated with the increasing focus on the credibility or otherwise of an applicant's account (Crawley 2007). One way forward would be to build a 'case conference' into the assessment process. This would ensure that all of the people involved in a particular case, including the age disputed applicant, sit down together and discuss the basis of the decision that has been reached. An independent third party should be present at any case conference, one of whose duties will be to ensure that the child or young person's interests are represented and that the process is conducted fairly and appropriately. The child or young person should also be allocated a guardian to assist him or her to negotiate the process and represent his or her best interests as appropriate. Where there are ongoing disagreements, these should be the subject of an independent review of the process by which the decision about an asylum seeker's age has been reached. The review will require that statutory guidance is established against which the quality of the assessment process can be measured. The review could be undertaken by the independent age assessment panel, the local authority ombudsman or a third party as appropriate. Establishing an independent review process would minimise the use of the courts, which is expensive, adversarial and not available to those without legal advice and representation. This would also contribute to improvements in the process of age assessment over the longer term.

In the meantime the debate about which agency should have primary responsibility for age assessments continues to be played out in the judicial system. Many doubt the local authorities' ability to be neutral in carrying out age assessments because of the resource implications; in effect local authorities have a vested interest in the outcome (Brownlees and Finch 2010). In addition, it is suggested that many social workers lack confidence in their own skills in conducting age assessments (Brownlees and Finch 2010; Crawley 2007). According to an evaluation report of the *London Safeguarding Trafficked Children Toolkit*, the issue of age assessments remains controversial for social work child protection and asylum teams, which is not a surprising finding. However, the pilot authorities felt strongly that decisions about age are best made through social interaction and social work assessment (London SCB 2011). This emphasis on improving the process of age assessment undertaken by social workers differs from the stated position of UKBA to develop 'specialist regional centres' where 'there will be a more consistent approach' (Home Office 2008, para. 5.3). This approach was formulated in response to the research produced by ILPA and its recommendations, but has proved difficult to implement because of the failure of the UASC reform programme, which was presented by the Home Office as a mechanism for delivering more specialist and concentrated services for separated asylum seeking children (Home Office 2008). In this context it appears that the most appropriate way forward would be to significantly improve the quality of training and support provided to both UKBA case owners and social workers in relation to the process of age assessment and to establish statutory guidance for local authorities to ensure consistency in procedures for assessing age and the use of medical and other evidence.

References

Bhabha, J. and Finch, N. (2006) *Seeking Asylum Alone: Unaccompanied and Separated Children and Refugee Protection in the UK*. Harvard, MA: Harvard Committee on Human Rights. Accessed on 31 May 2011 at www.ilpa.org.uk/seeking%20asylum%20alone.pdf

Brownlees, L. and Finch, N. (2010) *Levelling the Playing Field*. London: UNICEF.

Children's Commissioner for England (CCE) (2008) *Claiming Asylum at a Screening Unit as an Unaccompanied Child*. London: CCE. Accessed on 31 May 2011 at www.statewatch.org/news/2008/mar/uk-claiming-asylum-screening-unit.pdf

Children's Legal Centre (2003) *Information Note on The Queen on the application of B v Merton London Borough Council [2003] EWHC 1689 (Admin), [2003]*. Accessed on 31 May 2011 at www.childrenslegalcentre.com/Resources/CLC/Documents/PDF%20A-M/Merton%20Note.pdf.

Council of Europe (2005) *Convention on Action against Trafficking in Human Beings.* Warsaw: COE.

Crawley, H. (2007) *When is a Child Not a Child? Asylum, Age Disputes and the Process of Age Assessments.* London: ILPA. Accessed on 31 May 2011 at www.ilpa.org.uk/publications/ILPA%20Age%20 Dispute%20Report.pdf

Crawley, H. (2010) '"No one gives you a chance to say what you are thinking": Finding space for children's agency in the asylum system'. *Area 42,* 2, 162–169.

Crawley, H. (2011) 'Asexual, apolitical beings: The interpretation of children's identities and experiences in the UK asylum system'. *Journal of Ethnic and Migration Studies 378,* 1171–1184.

Home Office (2002) *Secure Borders, Safe Haven: Integration with Diversity in Modern Britain.* London: Home Office.

Home Office (2008) *Better Outcomes: The Way Forward. Improving the Care of Unaccompanied Asylum Seeking Children.* London: Home Office (BIA).

Home Office (undated) *Assessing Age: Asylum Process Guidance.* London:UKBA. Accessed on 31 May 2011 at www.ukba.homeoffice.gov.uk/sitecontent/documents/policyandlaw/ asylumprocessguidance/specialcases/

IND and ADSS (2004) *Age Assessment: Joint Working Protocol Between Immigration and Nationality Directorate of the Home Office (IND) and Association of Directors of Social Services (ADSS) for UK Local Government and Statutory Childcare Agencies.* London, IND and ADSS.

IND and ADSS (2006) *Age Assessment Joint Working Protocol between Immigration and Nationality Directorate (IND) and Association of Directors of Social Services (ADSS).* Accessed on 31 May 2011 at www.childrenslegalcentre.com/Migrant+Childrens+Project/Resources/ageassessment

Joint Committee on Human Rights (2007) *The Treatment of Asylum Seekers: Tenth Report of Session 2006-7,* London: The Stationery Office. Accessed on 31 May 2011 at www.publications.parliament. uk/pa/jt200607/jtselect/jtrights/81/81i.pdf_

Kelly, E. (2009) *Bordering on Concern: Child Trafficking in Wales.* Swansea: Children's Commissioner for Wales and ECPAT UK. Accessed on 31 May 2011 at www.ecpat.org.uk/content/ecpat-uk-reports

London SCB (2011) *Final Monitoring Report Local Authority Pilots of the London Safeguarding Trafficked Children Guidance and Toolkit.* London: London SCB. Accessed on 31 May 2011 at www. londonscb.gov.uk/trafficking/

Nandy, L. (2007) *Going it Alone: Children in the Asylum Process.* London: Children's Society.

R (B) v Merton London Borough Council [2003] EWHC 1689 (Admin), [2003] 4 All ER 280.

R (on the application of NA) v London Borough of Croydon [2009] EWHC 2357 (Admin). United Kingdom: High Court (England and Wales).

R (PM) v Hertfordshire County Council [2010] EWHC 2056 (Admin).

Royal College of Paediatrics and Child Health (RCPCH) (2003) *Assessment of the Age of Refugee Children.* Accessed on 31 May 2011 at www.rcpch.ac.uk/sites/default/files/Assessment_Age_ Refugee_Children.pdf

Royal College of Radiologists (2007) Letter to UKBA dated 23.05.2007. Accessed on 31 May 2011 at www.rcr.ac.uk/docs/general/pdf/AsylumseekersRCRfinalresponse.pdf

Separated Children in Europe Programme (SCEP) (2010) *Statement of Good Practice: Separated Children in Europe Program,* 4th edn. Denmark: Save the Children.

United Kingdom Border Agency (UKBA) (undated) *Assessing Age: Instructions for Case Owners.* Accessed on 20 July 2011 at www.ukba.homeoffice.gov.uk/sitecontent/documents/policyandlaw/ asylumprocessguidance/specialcases/guidance/assessing-age?view=Binary

Chapter Four

Safe Accommodation for Separated Children

Hannah Pearce

Introduction

The safe accommodation of separated children is vital to their well-being; however, for a number of reasons these children have been particularly disadvantaged in relation to accommodation provision. A number of obstacles have prevented their safe accommodation, leading to high rates of children going missing, inappropriate care provision from the local authority and children being treated as adults (Crawley 2007). At the heart of many of these disputes is the assessment and decision making around the age of a child. Without documentary proof of age, many separated children are age assessed by the local authority, a process which forms the basis for decisions about whether the individual should be treated as an adult or as a child. The structure of local authority service provision has made this a critical barrier for young people; if assessed as over 18, they may be accommodated with other adults, detained in preparation for dispersal or if EU migrants they may be asked to return to their country of origin. While the core theme of lack of provision applies to all separated children, this chapter looks primarily at the experiences of trafficked children, based on empirical research, their rights to accommodation, the risk of these children going missing and the current responses to accommodating them (Beddoe 2007; Kelly 2009).

Children are trafficked to the UK from a wide range of countries to be exploited in a variety of ways, including sexual exploitation, domestic servitude and other forms of forced labour (e.g. cannabis production), benefit fraud and forced criminality (e.g. pick-pocketing, begging and theft). These children are highly vulnerable and in need of wide ranging support, including medical and psychological care, legal assistance and education. Fundamental to this provision of care is the need for trafficked children to be provided with safe accommodation to enable recovery from the abuse they have faced, prevent them from facing further abuse, allow for their continued development and to provide young people with the rights that were denied them as victims of trafficking. Safe accommodation is defined for the purposes of this chapter as foster placements with foster carers who have received additional training in the care of children who may have been trafficked.

What is trafficking?

The accepted definition of human trafficking is taken from the UN *Protocol to Prevent, Suppress and Punish Trafficking in Persons, Especially Women and Children, Supplementing the UN Convention against Transnational Organized Crime* (United Nations 2000), commonly known as the Palermo Protocol.

> Trafficking in persons shall mean the recruitment, transportation, transfer, harbouring or receipt of persons, by means of the threat or use of force or other forms of coercion, of abduction, of fraud, of deception, of the abuse of power or of a position of vulnerability or of the giving or receiving of payments or benefits to achieve the consent of a person having control over another person, for the purpose of exploitation. (UN 2000, Article 3)

Significantly the means of trafficking such as threats, coercion, deception or abuse included in the definition of adult trafficking are not relevant to child trafficking because children cannot consent to their exploitation. Many children (and their families) are deceived by traffickers with promises of a better life and improved access to education, employment and a better standard of living in the UK. Children may agree to travel for the purposes of work or to live with another family, not realising that they will be exploited. Once children have been trafficked, they are especially vulnerable because they may have been coached or groomed by their trafficker to be fearful of authority and threatened with dire consequences if they do not comply or they may feel unable to challenge what an adult tells them. Children often believe they must support their family, which can leave them vulnerable to debt bondage, where their labour is demanded as a means of repayment to their traffickers.

Child trafficking is a hidden and complex crime and it is difficult to put an exact figure on the number of children trafficked in the UK. There is no formal coordination of information held by local authorities, police services, the United Kingdom Border Agency (UKBA) and other bodies to provide comprehensive statistics on child trafficking in the UK. There are, however, some indicative data available. In 2010, the Child Exploitation and Online Protection Centre published its third report on child trafficking in the UK, the *Strategic Threat Assessment – Child Trafficking in the UK*, which identified a total of 287 children from 47 countries as potential victims of trafficking (CEOP 2010). It is important to note that CEOP highlights the many limitations on the data gathered, including the size of the dataset, which was smaller than for previous comparable studies due to a reduction in resources and a tighter timescale. CEOP also suggests the research may be incomplete because of the way that trafficking offences are recorded by police (sometimes under a different type of offence), low awareness of trafficking and practical difficulties in retrieving information about cases which are not stored centrally (CEOP 2010). The UK Human Trafficking Centre (UKHTC), which has become part of the Serious and Organised Crime Agency, has provided some statistics collected from the National Referral Mechanism (NRM) for victims of trafficking – the government system for the identification of victims of trafficking (SOCA 2010). According to these data from 1 April 2009 until 30 June 2010, 215 children from 33 countries were referred into the NRM. However, these figures do not include those children who are unknown to the authorities, or who have not been identified as trafficked children, or who have simply not been referred into the NRM because the local authority is unaware of the system or does not believe the child would benefit from the referral. The true number of trafficked children in the UK is therefore likely to be far higher than these statistics suggest.

This lack of comprehensive data is a significant obstacle to understanding the scope of the problem and in planning an effective response to provide services to trafficked children. In recent years the UK government has made some progress in combating child trafficking by introducing legislation to prosecute and convict traffickers and improve safeguarding procedures for children who may have been trafficked. However, there are still barriers preventing child victims of trafficking from accessing essential services such as safe accommodation and there are significant gaps in the knowledge and understanding of those key professionals who are likely to encounter child victims of trafficking in the course of their work (Kelly 2009; Pearce, Hynes and Bovarnick 2009). Trafficked children will often first be identified as unaccompanied asylum seeking children; however, not all trafficked children are subject to immigration control and may be European Economic Area (EEA) nationals. It is crucial for professionals to be able to recognise possible indicators of trafficking whatever the nationality of the child.

Children who have been trafficked may have experienced prolonged exposure to abuse and neglect and due to the physical and psychological impact of this trauma need a high level of care and protection (Zimmerman *et al.* 2006). Research by End Child Prostitution, Child Pornography and the Trafficking of Children for Sexual Purposes (ECPAT UK) and its work with trafficked children have identified significant protection needs for children likely to be suffering from fear and anxiety, as well as physical manifestations of abuse (Beddoe 2007; Kelly 2009). In order for these children to receive the necessary care and support, they first need to be identified as trafficked by those professionals who come into contact with them, which means training on child trafficking is an essential requirement. Once identified, trafficked children require appropriate accommodation. Through ECPAT UK's experience of working with trafficked children, we suggest that the following considerations should be made. First, children should be consulted as to what emotional, physical and environmental factors would help them to feel safe; this may constitute physical factors such as locks and location but could just as well involve emotional needs that will help them to feel secure. Second, trafficked children should be cared for by individuals who have received specialist training to understand the experiences and needs of trafficked children, and who are available 24 hours a day providing the possibility to develop personal relationships. Third, the accommodation should be provided alongside access to education and appropriate healthcare necessary for the health and well-being of children who have experienced trauma and violence. ECPAT UK believe that for most children who have been trafficked, foster placements with trained foster carers provide the most appropriate form of accommodation.

International obligations to accommodate child victims of trafficking

There are a range of obligations under international and domestic law relevant to providing care and accommodation to separated children as a whole with some specific provisions for trafficked children. The United Nations (1989) Convention on the Rights of the Child obliges States to take positive action to protect children from all forms of exploitation and sexual abuse prejudicial to any aspect of their welfare. Under this convention, a child is considered to be anyone under the age of 18. Article 20 of the UNCRC states that a

> child temporarily or permanently deprived of his or her family environment, or in whose own best interests cannot be allowed

to remain in that environment, shall be entitled to special protection and assistance provided by the State. States Parties shall in accordance with their national laws ensure alternative care for such a child. Such care could include, inter alia, foster placement, kafalah of Islamic law, adoption or if necessary placement in suitable institutions for the care of children.

Article 6 of the Palermo Protocol states that 'child victims have the right to receive immediate care and protection including security, food, and accommodation in a safe place, access to social and health services, psychosocial support, legal assistance and education' (United Nations 2000). International and regional human rights principles form the basis of the UNICEF (2006) *Guidelines on the Protection of Child Victims of Trafficking*, which were developed in order to set out standards for good practice to protect and assist child victims of trafficking. The guidelines give an overview of measures for implementing appropriate policy and practice to protect and assist child victims of trafficking. Guideline 7.2 refers to accommodation in a safe place: 'Child victims shall be in safe and suitable accommodation immediately after their identification.' The 2000 Optional Protocol to the UNCRC on the Sale of Children, Child Prostitution and Child Pornography was developed to provide more detailed obligations regarding the protection of child victims of sexual exploitation, including trafficking. The UK became a State Party to the UNCRC in December 1991 and ratified the Optional Protocol in 2009.

The Council of Europe (2005) Convention on Action against Trafficking in Human Beings, which the UK ratified in 2009, contains various provisions specific to children regarding their protection and assistance: Article 10 states that child victims should receive 'special protection measures' and Article 12 states that 'appropriate and secure accommodation' should be provided. The Convention confirms that procedures concerning children must be different from those concerning adults. The UK is thus obligated under a range of international conventions to recognise the specific needs of trafficked children and provide accommodation accordingly in addition to the UK's own domestic safeguarding framework and duties.

Domestic obligations to accommodate child victims of trafficking

Professionals must be able to respond to a wide variety of indicators of trafficking, including trafficking for sexual exploitation, forced labour, domestic servitude and forced marriage. There is the risk that if the safeguarding intervention is not immediate, the young person will remain under the control of the trafficker, within an exploitative situation. The failure of authorities to identify these children as at risk of significant harm leaves them highly vulnerable to continued and further abusive experiences.

It is clear from ECPAT UK's work, as well as that of others including the National Society for the Prevention of Cruelty to Children (NSPCC) (Pearce *et al.* 2009) and UNICEF (Brownlees and Finch 2010), that trafficked children may fail to benefit from local authority services because practitioners may lack knowledge of the policy and procedures for trafficked children, their complex needs and the complicating factors of their immigration status. In addition, the absence of an independent advocate, sometimes called a guardian, who can act on their behalf and support children through the often confusing and bureaucratic care system can create further complications (see Chapter 9 for more details).

Once identified, trafficked children should be assessed by local authority children's services to determine the level of support and accommodation they require. The Children Act 1989 and 2004 set out the legal framework for all children 'in need' in England and Wales, with the Children (Scotland) Act (1995) establishing similar criteria. Crucially, under these Acts, the nationality or immigration status of the child should not affect agencies' statutory responsibilities. Where a young person, such as an unaccompanied asylum seeking child or accompanied child found to be living with an unknown adult, presents to a local authority as having no parent or guardian in the UK, the local authority will assess the child's circumstances and may conclude that it should accommodate the young person using its powers under Section 20 of the Children Act 1989. In these circumstances, the local authority will have legal duties and responsibilities towards the young person as a looked after child. In 2010 there were approximately 90,000 children looked after by local authorities in the UK, 3400 of the 64,400 looked after children in England at 31 March 2010 were unaccompanied asylum seeking children (DfE 2010).

While this process may seem straightforward, the reality for many separated and trafficked children is that they do not receive appropriate accommodation, with many children being accommodated in bed and breakfast type provision or mixed hostels. The dangers of such provision are manifold, including social isolation, lack of practical and emotional support, and no safeguards to prevent traffickers re-establishing contact with the young person (see Case 4.1). The issue of misinterpretation of the Children Act 1989, with children being provided with shelter under Section 17, led in 2003 to the Hillingdon Judgment, which ruled that 'the act of providing accommodation made the child looked after by the

Local Authority under Section 20' (Refugee Council 2007, p.2). Further guidance states that

> where a child has no parent or guardian in this country, perhaps because he has arrived alone seeking asylum, the presumption should be that he would fall within the scope of Section 20 and become looked after, unless the needs assessment reveals particular factors which would suggest that an alternative response would be more appropriate. (DoH 2003, p.3)

Case 4.1: Dalal's experience of living in unsupported accommodation

Dalal is a young person from China, who went missing in Wales. Dalal was given away as a child to foster parents because she was female and then sold to a Chinese female trafficker, who kept her locked up with many other girls. Dalal was then passed on to a man who took her on a ship to another destination, where she was passed on to another man. This man kept Dalal locked up for some time; he did not harm her but she was made to watch videos of children being beaten. This man then took her to the UK by plane and warned her to tell anyone who asked her age that she was 21, and that if she did not, she would be returned to China. When they arrived at Heathrow, Dalal hid in the lavatories until she was found by security. Dalal had a passport with her which stated that she was 21 years old; however, she claimed to be 16.

Dalal was treated as an adult by UKBA and was sent to a city in Wales, where she was placed in initial Home Office accommodation. Soon afterwards, Dalal was required to move to another city in Wales by UKBA and was placed in accommodation with several adult females. Voluntary sector agencies were concerned at her history and current vulnerabilities. At least three referrals were made to the local authority social work team and to the police.

Then, it was reported that Dalal had a man staying with her in the accommodation. The housing manager went to investigate and found a Chinese man hiding in her wardrobe. Dalal claimed that he was her brother, but it is thought by at least one of the voluntary agencies involved that he was the trafficker. Shortly afterwards, Dalal disappeared and is now officially recorded as a missing person.

Subsequent rulings have further supported the provision of accommodation to separated children because they fulfil the criteria under Section 20 of the Children Act 1989, although practice among local authorities remains varied (Pearce *et al.* 2009; Refugee Council 2007).

One of the rights bestowed on a child if accommodated under Section 20 is the right to leaving care support to help a young person through the transition process with plans that should be in place within three months of a child's 16th birthday. The Pathway Plan should reflect the young person's needs and how the local authority plans to support him or her towards independence. The level of support will depend on the length of time the child was looked after. Leaving care support is provided until the young person turns 21 (or 23 years for a child with a disability), although some support may continue to a maximum age of 24 (or 25 years for a child with a disability) if the young person continues to pursue a programme of education or training set out in his or her Pathway Plan. Separated children may have missed out on years of education because of their circumstances in their country of origin and their exploitative situation; their development may have been impeded in many other ways. These vulnerabilities are compounded by the fact that they will often lack any family or support network.

If there is a specific risk of significant harm to the child, for example if he or she were to be found with a trafficker, then safeguarding procedures under Section 47 of the Children Act 1989 would be followed and investigations made. If there is reasonable cause to believe that the child is suffering or likely to suffer significant harm, the child can be accommodated on a voluntary basis or an Emergency Protection Order (EPO) may be sought by the local authority or by the police powers under Section 46 of the Children Act 1989 to safeguard a child in England. The responsibilities of each agency and the mechanisms for multi-agency working are provided for in the guidance *Working Together to Safeguard Children* in England (DCSF 2010), *Safeguarding Children: Working Together under the Children Act 2004* in Wales (Welsh Assembly 2004) and *Protecting Children – A Shared Responsibility: Guidance on Inter-Agency Co-operation* in Scotland (Scottish Office 1998), which is currently being revised. Supplementary guidance regarding trafficked children has been produced in three of the four nations, beginning in 2007 with England's *Safeguarding Children Who May Have Been Trafficked* (DCSF 2007, revised 2011), followed in Wales in 2008 and in Scotland in 2009.

Further assessment by the local authority may conclude that it is necessary for the young person to be accommodated under Section 31 of the Children Act 1989, when an interim or full Care Order is issued by the courts. To issue a Care Order, the court must be satisfied that the child concerned 'is suffering or is likely to suffer significant harm, and that the harm, or likelihood of harm is attributable to the care given to the child, or likely to be given to him if the order were not made, or the care not being reasonable, or if the child is beyond parental control' (Children Act 1989, Section 31, 2). Once an interim Care Order is made, the local authority obtains parental responsibility in addition to the other parental responsibility holders. It should be noted that very few separated or trafficked children have been made subject to an interim or full Care Order, although in the case of very young children, such as the baby trafficked from Kenya by Peace Sandberg, the option of adoption proceedings is available.

Government guidance, *Safeguarding Children Who May Have Been Trafficked* (DoE 2011), states that the assessment of needs to inform the Care Plan should be the same as for any other looked after child. However, the guidance also covers special additional considerations for child victims of trafficking:

> 5.62 In addition, for children who may have been trafficked, the assessment should include: establishing relevant information about the child's background; understanding the reasons the child has come to the UK; and assessing the child's vulnerability to the continuing influence/control of his or her traffickers and the risks that they will go missing.
>
> 5.63 Responding to this information ensures that the care plan includes a risk assessment setting out how the local authority intends to safeguard the young person so that, as far as possible, they can be protected from any trafficker to minimise any risk of traffickers being able to reinvolve a child in exploitative activities. This plan should include contingency plans to be followed if the young person goes missing.
>
> 5.64 Given the circumstances in which potentially trafficked young people present to local authorities it will be extremely important that any needs assessments and related risk assessments are sensitively managed. It should allow for the child's need to be in a safe place before any assessment takes place and for the possibility that they may not be able to disclose full information about their circumstances immediately as they, or their families, may have been intimidated by traffickers. (DoE 2011, pp.29–30)

This guidance has been further expanded by the *London Safeguarding Trafficked Children Toolkit* produced by the London SCB (2011), which includes an assessment framework, matrix of risk indicators and information about trafficking. A pilot programme was run during 2009–2010 to monitor and trial the toolkit and was formally evaluated in early 2011. Children's services departments from 12 local authorities took part across the UK. The toolkit is used as a basis for making decisions to refer children suspected of being trafficked to the NRM and was launched nationally in early 2011.

The 2010 Court of Appeal judgment R (on the application of SO) v London Borough of Barking and Dagenham [2010] EWCA contains two important decisions for 'former relevant children' (which is a young person who was provided with accommodation by social services (i.e. a 'looked after child') pursuant to Section 20 of the Children Act 1989 for 13 weeks or more while still under 18 and to whom the local authority social services department now owes a range of leaving care duties) or care leavers. The judgment stated that, first, local authorities have a general duty to provide a former relevant child with accommodation to the extent that his or her welfare requires it. Second, in considering whether a former relevant child's welfare requires the provision of accommodation, the local authority is not permitted to take account of whether or not that former relevant child might be eligible for accommodation and support from the Home Office pursuant to its asylum support functions (previously carried out by the National Asylum Support Service and generally still referred to as NASS). This judgment means that if a former relevant child is unable to access appropriate accommodation through some other means (such as through a combination of a council tenancy and housing benefit), and the provision of accommodation is necessary for that young person's welfare, then social services will be under a duty to provide or arrange suitable accommodation. The type of accommodation required will depend on the individual's needs, which should be identified in the Pathway Plan, but could range from some form of specialist residential placement, to continuation of a foster placement, or the arranging of a tenancy and payment of the rent deposit. This duty will apply from the outset when the young person turns 18, but it could also apply if the young person has accessed some other form of accommodation, and then loses it while still a former relevant child. Significantly the Court of Appeal found that a local authority is not entitled, when considering whether a former relevant child's welfare requires that he or she be accommodated by it, to take account of the possibility of support from NASS. This means that on turning 18, it is not permissible for the local authority to send former unaccompanied asylum seeking minors to be accommodated by NASS. As asylum seekers and failed asylum seekers are not able to work or to access mainstream benefits and housing, the practical effect of this is that it will fall to local authorities to continue to provide accommodation and support to former relevant children who are asylum seekers or failed asylum seekers until the age of 21 (or 24 if the young person is pursuing a programme of education or training).

Children who have been trafficked

ECPAT UK has worked with a number of children who have been trafficked and who have received inadequate accommodation. Because trafficked children are extremely vulnerable, ECPAT UK has repeatedly called for foster care to be provided for all children suspected to have been trafficked as the most appropriate form of accommodation that can provide the intensive support and supervision needed. Crucially foster care provides the opportunity for the child to create personal relationships with appropriate warmth and affection in a stable, safe environment. Too many child victims of trafficking are provided with inappropriate accommodation such as bed and breakfast accommodation or hostels. Trafficked children require a safe and supportive environment that affords them protection from their abusers. ECPAT UK believes the best option for child victims of trafficking is for them to be placed with foster carers who have received specialist training on the specific needs of trafficked children and on the risks that they face. Such placements need to be provided with a robust risk assessment and a support network of professionals who have both the knowledge and experience of working with trafficked children. Careful consideration also needs to be given to where (geographically) a child is placed. To ensure their safety, children may well need to be accommodated in a different local authority from the location they were kept by their traffickers.

Going missing

ECPAT UK's research has previously highlighted the significant numbers of children who go missing from care. In 2007, the study *Missing Out* (Beddoe 2007) found 60 per cent of children suspected of being victims of trafficking had subsequently gone missing from local authority care. The CEOP (2010) report found that 18 per cent (53) of the children identified in the study were recorded as having gone missing from local authority accommodation at some point, with 15 per cent (42) still recorded as missing and that most victims had gone missing within one week, many within 48 hours. Freedom of information requests in 2009 found that 173 unaccompanied asylum seeking children went missing from Kent County Council care, 21 from Leicestershire and 20 from Bedfordshire in 2009 (BBC Radio 4 2010). Exact figures for asylum seeking children missing from care are not available, as the UK government does not centrally collect the number of looked after children who may have been trafficked into the UK and who have subsequently gone missing from care.

ECPAT UK's research revealed that the high numbers of trafficked children who go missing may still be under the control of traffickers while in the care of the local authority and disappear because the trafficker has regained control over them, or that they have run away for fear of being found by the trafficker. In both scenarios the children are in highly vulnerable and potentially dangerous situations. The revised *Statutory Guidance on Children who Run Away and go Missing from Home or Care* (DCSF 2009) provides further procedures on minimising risk of going missing but does not offer much guidance on actual prevention. Secure accommodation is often mentioned as a possible way to safeguard children who are at risk of being taken back by their traffickers. While it would be disproportionate to accommodate a child in secure accommodation which would conflict with the child's freedom of movement, safeguards (which are discussed below) can be introduced to minimise the risk of the child going missing.

Age assessment

A significant complicating factor in accommodating trafficked children, as with all separated children, can sometimes be caused by a lack of their documented age and the need to assess their age in order to identify appropriate levels of care and support. The outcomes of age assessments have a significant impact on local authority resources, yet the local authority is expected to objectively assess the age of a child in the knowledge that broadly speaking the younger a child is assessed, the greater the financial burden is likely to be on the local authority.

Children who may have been trafficked will often have no identification documents, may have false documents, or will have been instructed by their traffickers to lie about their age. If children are is disputed by the local authority, this can prevent the child being provided with appropriate support and accommodation until the age dispute is settled. If children are initially thought to be over 18 years, they are likely to be temporarily accommodated in bed and breakfast facilities or treated as adults seeking asylum, which can lead to them being moved across the UK (Brownlees and Finch 2010). For some children, disputed age assessments have led to them being detained (Bhabha and Finch 2006). The difference in quality and type of care provided to a child while the age assessment is being undertaken is also variable. ECPAT UK believes that when disputes arise, age should be assessed by an independent panel with expertise in child and adolescent development and who have been trained in child-appropriate interview techniques. While acknowledging the difficulties in accurately assessing age when a child's age is in question, the local authority should give the child the 'benefit of the doubt'; this provision is reinforced by Article 10.3 of the Council of Europe Convention on Trafficking (see Case 4.2).

Case 4.2: Evelyn's experience of being forced to live in adult accommodation

One young person whom ECPAT UK has recently worked with was originally referred to the local authority by the police. She was treated as an adult even though she said she was 15; she was placed in NASS accommodation with other adults. She was very vulnerable and had been exploited through domestic servitude where she had rarely left the house. While she was living in NASS accommodation, a young man approached her and said he would help her; he told her she was his girlfriend and had sex with her. She became pregnant and now has a child. Eventually her solicitor requested an age assessment, which determined that she was 15 and she was then placed in foster care. If social services had used the benefit of the doubt principle, she would have been immediately placed in foster care and would have received greater protection. This very vulnerable young person in need of help was failed by the system meant to provide her with protection.

Current practice

There are some examples of good practice by local authorities who have responded effectively to trafficked children in their care and implemented specific policies to address their particular needs. The London Borough of Hounslow, where the Unaccompanied Minors Team has received training to safeguard children who may have been trafficked, and accommodates such children in foster care or semi-independent care; children under 16 are automatically placed in foster care. A needs assessment is carried out if the child is over 16; if a child has particular needs such as vulnerability as a victim of trafficking, the local authority will try to place the child in appropriate foster care. Similarly, Harrow Council has published guidance for social care, education professionals, foster carers and residential staff (Harrow Council 2010). This guidance suggests actions to be taken to minimise the risk of the child going missing, including taking a photograph of the child, providing close adult supervision and considering removal of the child's mobile phone or SIM card. The guidance further states that foster care or residential care may be considered for the child and that the foster carers or residential staff should have an awareness of trafficking and the impact on victims. A needs and risk assessment should be conducted to determine the level of adult supervision required.

Hertfordshire local authority has developed an anti-trafficking project in response to an increased number of young Vietnamese boys being referred to children's services and subsequently going missing in early 2009. Hertfordshire's children's services are working closely with Hertfordshire Constabulary and have trained a number of social workers on trafficking issues to enable the police to call one of these designated social workers if they discover a child they suspect of being trafficked (Hertfordshire Anti-Trafficking Project 2010). The child is then placed with foster carers.

The London Borough of Hillingdon has introduced good practice guidelines for working with trafficked children, which includes residential guidance (Hillingdon 2010). This has been successful in significantly reducing the number of trafficked children who go missing from their care following media reports of 77 Chinese children going missing from Hillingdon's care in 2007 (Booth 2009). In evidence to the Home Affairs Select Committee in 2009, Hillingdon reported four Chinese children missing from care in the previous year, a significant decrease. The protocol includes increased supervision of the child, restricted and monitored use of mobile phones, email and the internet, together with improved confidentiality of the location of placements.

Operation Newbridge was established in West Sussex in 2008 to respond to concerns developed over several years about a number of children who arrived at Gatwick Airport and shortly afterwards went missing (CEOP 2010). These young people, of Chinese and West African origin, were believed to be victims of trafficking and taken into local authority care, but subsequently went missing. Newbridge was set up as a multi-agency response involving the airport, UKBA, social services and the police. The aim is to create a barrier in communication between the child and the trafficker, for example, no unsupervised visits to the child's accommodation and limited access to phones or the internet. Newbridge works with a private accommodation provider that provides residential care for unaccompanied asylum seeking children and offers a protection plan for any young person who is thought to have been trafficked into the UK. Children thought to be at risk of being trafficked are placed on a voluntary 24-hour protection plan organised by children's services where the child is accompanied by a member of staff at all times. The child is not allowed to use a phone and cannot contact anyone without a member of staff being informed. The plan runs for four weeks but is constantly reviewed to take any new information into account. Greater security is provided to child victims of trafficking by not accommodating them on the ground floor and by the use of sensory motion alarms and CCTV. This support is bolstered by sessions with key workers where the children learn independent living skills. The independent review of Operation Newbridge has yet to be published but its progress has demonstrated successful multi-agency working that has ensured that all the different agencies involved prioritise safeguarding. There is also evidence to suggest that Operation Newbridge has had a preventative effect: numbers of children arriving who are thought to be at risk of trafficking have reduced significantly, although this may mean the problem has simply been displaced, with children being trafficked via airports other than Gatwick.

Conclusion

In order for trafficked children to be provided with the care and support they need, they must be identified as trafficked. Therefore, training and awareness is required for all practitioners who are likely to come into contact with a trafficked child. To achieve this a designated lead manager on child trafficking should be appointed in every local authority to ensure leadership, responsibility and direction. This recommendation is supported by *Working Together* (DCSF 2010), which states that at a local level, local safeguarding children boards should be aware of the child trafficking agenda within their local authority. The guidance calls for LSCBs to identify trafficking coordinators who can ensure a coordinated campaign of information-sharing to support the safeguarding agenda between local authorities, police and the NRM competent authorities to 'secure the best safeguarding outcome for the child'.

ECPAT UK's own experience is that trafficked children are likely to receive inadequate accommodation; however, this chapter has also described several examples of good practice in accommodating trafficked children, which takes into account their particular circumstances and needs. Where such specialist models have been developed, these may provide the best local alternative for children who have been trafficked. However, where a more specialist model is not available, as is the case in most parts of the UK, ECPAT UK recommends that foster care be provided for all children thought to have been trafficked as the most appropriate form of accommodation that can provide the intensive support and supervision needed for these children, who have a high level of complex needs.

References

BBC Radio 4 (2010) The Report – Child trafficking, BBC Radio 4 on 21/01/2010. Accessed on 31January 2011 at www.bbc.co.uk/programmes/b00pxslj

Beddoe, C. (2007) *Missing Out: A Study of Child Trafficking in the North-West, North-East and West Midlands.* London: ECPAT UK.

Bhabha, J. and Finch, N. (2006) *Seeking Asylum Alone Unaccompanied and Separated Children and Refugee Protection in the UK.* Harvard, MA: Macarthur Foundation.

Booth, R. (2009) 'Revealed: 77 trafficked Chinese children lost by home'. *The Guardian,* 5 May 2009.

Brownlees, L. and Finch, N. (2010) *Levelling the Playing Field.* London: UNICEF.

Child Exploitation and Online Protection Centre (CEOP) (2010) *Strategic Threat Assessment: Child Trafficking in the UK.* London: CEOP.

Council of Europe (2005) *Convention on Action against Trafficking in Human Beings.* Warsaw: COE.

Crawley, H. (2007) *When is a Child Not a Child? Asylum, Age Disputes and the Process of Age Assessment.* London: ILPA.

Department for Children, Schools and Families (DCSF) (2007) *Working Together to Safeguard Children – Safeguarding Children Who May Have Been Trafficked*

Department for Children, Schools and Families (DCSF) (2009) *Statutory Guidance on Children who Run Away and go Missing from Home or Care.* London: TSO.

Department for Children, Schools and Families (DCSF) (2010) *Working Together to Safeguard Children. A Guide to Inter-agency Working to Safeguard and Promote the Welfare of Children.* London: TSO.

Department of Education (DfE) (2010) *Children Looked After by Local Authorities in England (including adoption and care leavers) - year ending 31 March 2010.* Accessed on 11 October 2011 at www. education.gov.uk/rsgateway/DB/SFR/s000960/index.shtml.

Department for Education (DoE) (2011) *Working Together to Safeguard Children: Safeguarding Children Who May Have Been Trafficked.* Accessed on 31 October 2001 at www.education.gov.uk/publications/standard/publicationDetail/Page1/DFE-00084-2001.

Department of Health (2003) *Local Authority Circular (2003) 13: Guidance on Accommodating Children In Need and their Families.*

Harrow Council (2010) *Good Practice Guidance for Trafficked Children in Care.* London: London Borough of Harrow.

Hertfordshire Anti-Trafficking Project (2010) East of England Migration Impacts Fund Report 2009–2010. Accessed on 31 January 2011 at www.dacorumcvs.org.uk/downloads/MIF%20 report%202010.pdf

Hillingdon (2010) *Good Practice Guidance; Trafficked Children.* London: London Borough of Hillingdon.

Kelly, E. (2009) *Bordering on Concern: Child Trafficking in Wales.* Swansea: Children's Commissioner for Wales and ECPAT UK.

London SCB (2011) *Final Monitoring Report Local Authority Pilots of the London Safeguarding Trafficked Children Guidance and Toolkit.* London: London SCB.

Pearce, J., Hynes, P. and Bovarnick, S. (2009) *Breaking the Wall of Silence: Practitioners' Responses to Trafficked Children and Young People.* London: NSPCC.

R (on the application of SO) v London Borough of Barking and Dagenham [2010] EWCA Civ 1101.

Refugee Council (2007) *Determining the Duty to Look After Unaccompanied Children under the Children Act 1989 (use of section 17 or section 20).* Accessed on 31 January 2011 at www.refugeecouncil.org.uk/Resources/Refugee%20Council/downloads/briefings/wandsworthjudgment_briefing.pdf

Scottish Office (1998) *Protecting Children – A Shared Responsibility: Guidance on Inter-Agency Co-operation in Scotland.* Edinburgh: Scottish Office.

Serious Organised Crime Agency (SOCA) (2010) *National Referral Mechanism Statistical Data April 2009 to March 2010* Accessed on 31 January 2011 at www.soca.gov.uk/about-soca/about-the-ukhtc/statistical-data

UN Children's Fund (UNICEF) 2006 *Guidelines on the Protection of Child Victims of Trafficking.* Accessed on 31 January 2011 at: www.unhcr.org/refworld/docid/49997af727.html

United Nations (1989) *Convention on the Rights of the Child.* New York: United Nations.

United Nations (2000) *Protocol to Prevent, Suppress, and Punish Trafficking in Persons, Especially Women and Children, Supplementing the United Nations Convention against Transnational Organized Crime.* New York: General Assembly.

Welsh Assembly (2004) *Safeguarding Children: Working Together under the Children Act 2004.* Cardiff: Welsh Assembly.

Zimmerman, C., Hossain, M., Yun, K., Roche, B., Morrison, L. and Watts, C. (2006) *Stolen Smiles: The Physical and Psychological health Consequences of Women and Adolescents Trafficked into Europe.* London. London School of Hygiene and Tropical Medicine.

Chapter Five

Living with Unrelated Adults

Private Fostering

Catherine Shaw and Savita de Sousa

Introduction

There have been longstanding concerns about the welfare and potential vulnerability of children living in informal private arrangements with adults other than their parents or close family members. This dates back to the baby-farming scandals of the 19th century and continued through the mass evacuation of children during the Second World War (Holman 2002). By the 1990s the focus of such concerns rested principally on West African children living on a long-term basis with white carers, often in predominately white or rural areas, and with little or no regular contact with their birth parents (Utting 1997). The death of Victoria Climbié, a privately fostered child from the Ivory Coast living in England with a great-aunt, brought the issue of private fostering to wider public attention in 2000, and precipitated wide ranging changes to the way in which local authority children's services were structured and delivered. Nevertheless, 11 years later, the term 'private fostering' and its legal definition still remained largely unknown, and fears about the safety and well-being of children in such arrangements have not been assuaged.

In this chapter we describe the current legal and policy context, followed by a discussion of the specific challenges for practitioners and local authorities in relation to children from overseas living in private fostering arrangements. Case studies of four children are included as illustrative examples and we are grateful to staff from the British Association for Adoption and Fostering (BAAF) Northern Ireland, Newport City Council and the London Boroughs of Merton and Tower Hamlets, who kindly supplied the information upon which the case studies are based.

Private fostering and privately fostered children

Private fostering occurs when a child under 16 (or under 18 if the child has a disability) is cared for, and provided with accommodation, for 28 days or more by someone other than a close relative, guardian or someone with parental responsibility. Close relatives are defined in legislation as parents, stepparents, siblings, brothers or sisters of a parent, and grandparents, either full or half blood.

It is not known how many refugee, migrant or trafficked children are living in private fostering arrangements in the UK. Since 2004, the governments in England and Wales resumed collecting and publishing data from local authorities about privately fostered children. No comparable data is available for Scotland or Northern Ireland.

According to the most recent data available, as of 31 March 2010, a total of 1590 children were reported to be in private fostering arrangements in England, of whom 35 per cent were born outside the UK (this figure includes children visiting the UK for short-term educational purposes and those brought in with a view to adoption, as well as refugees, migrants and trafficked children). However, these data are of negligible value as they include only those arrangements known to the local authority and as such clearly underrepresents – and to an unknown extent – the true scale of private fostering.

The UK legislative and policy context

While the language is similar, private fostering is quite distinct from foster placements provided for looked after children. In the latter case, foster carers are recruited, assessed, trained and supported by the local authority, and the local authority is also involved in placing children with carers. By contrast, private fostering is initiated as a private arrangement made between parent and carer, in which the local authority has no initial involvement. Parental responsibility continues to reside with the parent, who in turn is expected to provide money for his or her child's upkeep. The regulations governing the arrangements for private foster care in the UK are outlined in the Foster Children (Scotland) Act 1984 (and the Foster Children (Private Fostering) (Scotland) Regulations 1985), Part X of the Children (Northern Ireland) Order 1995 (and the Children (Private Arrangements for Fostering) (Northern Ireland) 1996) and Part IX of the Children Act 1989 in Wales (and the Children (Private Arrangements for Fostering) Regulations 2006) and England (and the Children (Private Arrangements for Fostering) Regulations 2005). The regulations state that every local authority or trust shall satisfy itself that the welfare of children who are privately fostered within its area are being satisfactorily safeguarded and promoted and ensure that such advice is given to those caring for them as appears to the local authority or trust to be needed. The law aims to strike a balance between the duty of parents to exercise their responsibilities towards their children and the duty of the state to intervene to ensure that children's welfare is safeguarded and promoted.

In the wake of Victoria Climbié's death and the subsequent inquiry by Lord Laming (Department of Health and Home Office 2003), the Children Act 2004 (Section 44) introduced a tighter regulatory framework in England and Wales and a duty to cooperate through interagency collaboration to safeguard children and promote their welfare. The Children (Private Arrangements for Fostering) Regulations (2005 in England) (2006 in Wales) placed a duty on the local authority to promote public awareness of the notification requirements and to satisfy itself that the welfare of children who are proposed or are actually privately fostered is being satisfactorily safeguarded. Local authorities must also appoint an officer to monitor compliance with the notification system, and to report to the Director of Children's Services and the Local Safeguarding Children Board (LSCB).

The 2005 Regulations embody the key elements of the *Every Child Matters* reform programme in England and Wales (DfES 2004) in terms of prevention and early intervention. While designed to focus the attention of local authorities on private fostering, it is, however, not clear to what extent these priorities are currently being applied in practice. Privately fostered children are 'potentially children in need' (ADSS 2005) and there is a duty on all UK local authorities (or trusts in Northern Ireland) to safeguard and promote their welfare. Although this legal status is a useful lever for obtaining resources, research shows that services for children in need may be squeezed out by the demands of child protection work (Shaw *et al.* 2010).

In 2009 an Advisory Group on Private Fostering was set up to advise the Department for Children, Schools and Families (DCSF) to consider options for strengthening the notification system and the possibility of introducing registration for private foster carers. The Advisory Group concluded that the current system is proportionate and fit for purpose – if implemented effectively (Macleod 2010).

Characteristics of privately fostered children

It is clear from the definition of private fostering that it potentially applies to a wide variety of children living in a range of different circumstances.

The fact that a minimum, but no maximum, duration is stipulated means that the private fostering legislation covers children away from home for a relatively short period of time, to those living apart from their parents for many years. Babies and teenagers are equally included in the definition, and they may be separated from their parents by an ocean, or be staying just a few doors down the road. Some private foster carers will already be well known to the child, whereas others could be complete strangers.

Parents' reasons for making such arrangements may be equally diverse. Some have an essentially positive or optimistic foundation, including children being provided with short-term educational opportunities, or longer-term chances of a better life and improved future economic prospects. Other arrangements are born of necessity, for example if a parent is temporarily unable to look after his or her child due to illness, incarceration or employment circumstances. Teenagers in conflict with their parents may live for a while with the family of a friend until relationships improve.

Some of these children will be refugees, migrants or trafficked children, and may come to be in private fostering arrangements in a number of different ways, including the following:

- Children who arrive in the UK with a parent and subsequently enter into a private fostering arrangement, for example when the parent is deported or returns to his or her home country voluntarily, leaving the child in the care of a friend or distant relative. While some parents return, others may not be allowed back into the UK, and some effectively disappear, apparently abandoning their children.

- Children who are brought into the UK by a friend or distant relative from their own community or delivered into such an arrangement by an agent or courier. (These are unambiguous examples of private fostering arrangements, in that they were planned in advance by the child's parents. Victoria Climbié is an example of such a child.)

- Children brought in by an agent and subsequently abandoned to become unaccompanied children. Some children are reputedly 'found on the street' and 'taken in' by an adult from the same country or ethnic group.

- Children who are trafficked, for example being brought in for the purpose of domestic servitude or for sexual exploitation. (If the parent agreed to the child living with the adults concerned, legally this would be a private fostering arrangement.)

Practice challenges for local authorities

Private fostering presents a considerable challenge to local authorities; the range of responsibilities is wide, including raising awareness of the issue, assessing carers and their accommodation, regular monitoring of arrangements, and providing support as required to children, their parents and private foster carers, whose needs and circumstances vary widely. A dedicated private fostering team is a rarity, and in most authorities resources to carry out this work are very limited. Difficult choices have to be made, and discretion exercised. In this section we draw on research carried out by the National Children's Bureau (NCB) and the BAAF (Shaw *et al.* 2010) to outline some of the specific challenges and dilemmas facing local authorities and practitioners in identifying, assessing and supporting children from abroad living with private foster carers. Using data from a survey of private fostering practitioners, qualitative work carried out in eight local authorities and specific case studies of individual children submitted to BAAF, we are also able to highlight local responses to some of the complex situations presented.

Identifying privately fostered children

In order to carry out the statutory safeguarding assessments and follow-up visits, children's services must first be aware that a private fostering arrangement exists, or is proposed. According to the law, parents or private foster carers must notify the authorities in advance of any arrangement. However, our research revealed that this very rarely happens in practice. Rather, the vast majority of known private fostering arrangements are 'discovered' by practitioners rather than notified by the parties involved. It is thus assumed that an even larger number of such arrangements must remain unknown to the authorities; and the children living in such circumstances should be considered – until confirmed otherwise – to be vulnerable and potentially at risk.

One (benign) reason for the under-notification of private fostering arrangements is undoubtedly widespread ignorance about private fostering and the duty to notify. Such ignorance is endemic both among the general public (including those actually or potentially entering into such arrangements) and, perhaps more worryingly, among professionals who routinely come into contact with children and families through the course of their work. Thus some children are missing out on safeguarding checks and possible support simply because the adults in their lives do not recognise or understand the term 'private fostering'.

Of greater concern is that some arrangements are being hidden from the authorities. There may be various reasons for this, including a generalised distrust of statutory agencies (which in itself may be a result of negative experiences in their home countries or in the UK), because they actually 'have something to hide' (e.g. the arrangement is a cover for trafficking, exploitation or abuse) or because they themselves are fearful victims of human trafficking. While actual numbers of concealed arrangements are unknown, it is likely – for the reasons outlined above – that a high proportion of these hidden private fostering arrangements are those involving children from abroad.

Somewhere in between these two extremes lie situations in which individuals may have some awareness of private fostering law, but do not proactively inform the local authority. This may arise from a lack of understanding between the individuals and agencies involved. Within some cultures, where it is acceptable for children to be cared for by distant relatives or people unrelated to them, the need for local authority 'interference' is not always comprehended.

Nor is a lack of knowledge and confidence necessarily confined to the parents and carers involved in private fostering arrangements. Practitioners can be equally reluctant to get involved. When carrying out our research, we heard reports of teachers who were unwilling to enquire closely about the relationship between a child and carer for fear of being accused of racism, and of social workers who failed to fully challenge or probe when investigating possible private fostering arrangements out of 'respect' for cultural traditions. Nevertheless, some local authorities have had considerable success in gaining the trust and cooperation of their local communities, leading to increasing numbers of direct notifications of private fostering arrangements of children whose parents are abroad. These tend to be authorities with relatively large black and minority ethnic populations, making it easier to identify relevant community organisations with which to engage. For example, private fostering officers have, in some local authorities forged effective links with organisations supporting refugees, those that liaise with African or Muslim families, and the local Faith Forum. Direct contacts have been made with religious leaders including imams and pastors, leading to regular meetings and exchanges of information.

In order to build trust and cooperation, private fostering officers in these authorities avoid focusing on immigration status; indeed, some authorities appear to have unofficially adopted a 'don't ask, don't tell' policy. Instead they concentrate on safeguarding issues and accessing services for the child and carer. Workers often use Victoria Climbié as an example to justify the assessment and monitoring. Such an approach has reportedly led to greater trust within certain communities, and thanks to a 'ripple effect' over time, gradually increasing numbers of people coming forward to notify about their own private fostering arrangements.

However, direct notification remains a rarity and, in practice, local authorities tend to find out about private fostering only after the arrangements have been in place for some considerable time. The private fostering officer may be alerted by other practitioners who come across private fostering during the course of their work (such as a social worker investigating a 'child in need' case) or via agencies that have a protocol in place to refer suspected private fostering cases. All four case examples came to the attention of the local authority via other practitioners or agencies.

Case 5.1: Miele – an example of an asylum seeking child

Miele came to the attention of the local authority via the Home Office, which contacted them when his carer took him to make an application for asylum. This was thought to be a possible private fostering arrangement. Miele's carer claimed to have found him outside a fish and chip shop while buying dinner for her family. She stated that he was distressed and because they are from a similar ethnic background, she spoke to him and when she heard about his plight took pity and gave him shelter in her home. She did not inform anyone of this young person at the time and at a later date presented him to the Home Office.

Miele claimed to be an orphan who travelled to the UK from Bangladesh, following the death of both parents in a cyclone. Initially the local authority decided to accommodate Miele because there were a number of concerns with regard to the stated relationship between him and his carer and a worry that he was a trafficked young person. However, the level of distress displayed by Miele in his foster placement was suggestive of a closer than stated attachment to his initial carers. His carers also presented in a manner indicative of this. Furthermore, the carer instructed her legal representative to disclose that she was actually Miele's mother's sister. Following a robust interview at the Home Office, the carer instructed her legal representative to retract the statement.

Because of Miele's distress in his foster placement, the local authority decided to return him to his initial carers, who continued to maintain that they found him on the street and were not related to him. Accordingly, a private fostering core assessment was completed.

However, ongoing work with the family eventually led them to admit they are in fact direct members of this young person's family, as stated when he was first removed from their care. This admission was alongside a Home Office decision to instigate DNA testing.

The family maintain they contacted a solicitor because the young person, who had travelled to the UK on a tourist visa, overstayed and they wanted him to remain in the UK. They also claim that the solicitor provided them with a script/story to be used as part of an asylum claim. Although this is not technically a private fostering arrangement, the local authority is treating it as such.

For such referral systems to work, relevant practitioners need to have an understanding of private fostering, and it is part of the duty of local authorities to raise such awareness. Again this is a daunting task for often over-stretched private fostering officers, as the potential range of practitioners and agencies who may encounter private fostering in their day-to-day work is extremely broad, encompassing those who work in a range of services working specifically with adults (e.g. probation and prison services), those working generally within the community (e.g. general practitioners (GPs) and housing officers) as well as members of the children's workforce. Feedback from private fostering officers suggest that a carefully targeted approach is most effective, focusing on specific individuals or teams (e.g. GPs' receptionists or schools admissions officers) who, through their routine daily activities, are well placed to identify children who are not living with their parents.

Establishing the facts about possible private fostering arrangements

Once a suspected private fostering arrangement has been notified or reported to children's services, the local authority is required to assess the suitability of the carer and his or her accommodation, and ensure the well-being of the child. Another aspect of the assessment is to confirm that the arrangement really is one of private fostering under the legal definition. The case files of private fostering practitioners contain numerous ambiguous cases where arrangements are on the fringes of the law, including babies who are brought into the UK from abroad with a view to adoption, cases where relationships cannot readily be established and trafficking is suspected (see Case 5.1) children whose parents cannot be traced (see Cases 5.2 and 5.4), and unaccompanied asylum seekers (who should really be accommodated by the local authority).

Case 5.2: Pamela – an example of a child brought into the country by a distant relative

Pamela is a six-year-old girl from St Vincent who arrived in the UK in 2008, accompanied by a grandmother figure, understood to be her grandfather's sister. The carer subsequently applied for an extension to their holiday visa, alleging that Pamela's mother had absconded and her whereabouts were not known.

The arrangement came to the attention of the local authority when the carer contacted the schools admission service, seeking a school place for Pamela. The UK Border Agency's (UKBA) assumption was that the child should not access education due to no recourse to public funds. However, the local authority is committed to ensuring the welfare of any child, including provision of health and education, if Pamela is likely to stay in the UK. The carer currently has a visa extension and intends to apply for the child to remain indefinitely.

Pamela lives with her carer and members of the carer's extended family. Pamela sometimes spoke of her father and other members of her birth family, but this was not encouraged by her carer. Social workers concerned about attachment issues advised the carer to create a Life Story book with Pamela or compile albums of events and birth family members, although this wasn't pursued by her carer. It seems that the carer is reluctant to reveal too much about family relationships and ties for fear that Pamela will be returned to her birth family. Attachment issues are regularly dismissed by adults in Pamela's life as being 'Eurocentric methods'; their priorities are that she access a good education, health services and a positive future in the UK.

Nobody currently has parental responsibility for Pamela; the carer has been advised to seek parental responsibility via a Residence Order (an order from the court to say who Pamela should live with). In the meantime, this is being treated as a private fostering arrangement.

The '28 day rule' (whereby an arrangement counts as private fostering only if it is intended to last for more than 28 days) can also be problematic from a safeguarding point of view, potentially delaying intervention in situations where trafficking is suspected. It is not uncommon, for example, for a local authority informed of a possible private fostering situation by the UKBA to arrive at the address provided, only to find that the child is no longer there, or has never been there.

As the definition of private fostering hinges in part on the relationship between the carer and the child, this needs to be determined by the private fostering practitioner. This is often far from straightforward, particularly given cultural differences regarding the naming of kinship relationships, and what is considered to be 'close' family. Different legal frameworks in different countries regarding who is a legitimate carer or parent figure can further add to the confusion (see Case 5.3), as can deliberate deception to avoid deportation, as in Case 5.1.

Because of the complexities involved, some local authorities have now established private fostering panels to make decisions about individual cases, rather than leaving this to individual practitioners. In order to ensure that the child is safeguarded while their legal status is established, many practitioners adopt a 'safety first approach' whereby ambiguous or problematic cases are automatically 'treated as private fostering'. This may be a temporary designation pending further investigation, or may continue on a longer-term basis – even though the legal definition of private fostering has not been fully met – in order to ensure a minimum level of safeguarding oversight for the child (see Cases 5.1 and 5.2).

Immigration issues

Entrants to the UK with a question mark against their immigration status are generally investigated by the Home Office first, and until their status is established, clarification of their living arrangements (including whether or not it is a private fostering arrangement) may be put on hold. Private fostering practitioners feel that the delays caused by such procedures mean that children risk remaining in potentially dangerous situations for longer than necessary. Their cases illustrate the conflict between a child-centred system designed to both protect and secure children's welfare and the requirement on agencies to determine eligibility and ration expenditure of public resources (see Case 5.2). As a result, these children can find themselves in a dangerous limbo between the UK's safeguarding legislative framework and its immigration policy.

Keeping in contact with children, parents and carers

As private fostering is in essence an arrangement made willingly between the child's parent and the carer, the parent's views and intentions should be elicited as part of the assessment process. It is also necessary for the local authority to maintain communication with the parent, as he or she retains parental responsibility for his or her child for the duration of the private fostering arrangement; such responsibility may need to be exercised, for example if the child requires medical treatment.

Case 5.3: Sara – an example of a child brought into the country under a non-UK social care arrangement

Sara is a three-year-old girl who arrived in Northern Ireland in 2010 with her carers, a Lithuanian couple. The Southern Health and Social Care Trust was notified of the arrangement when Sara was taken to be registered at a GP practice.

There are no family links between Sara and her carers and she was placed with them by the Lithuanian authorities, following some time in institutional care. Lithuanian social services consider this to be the child's permanent placement and have given 'guardianship' to the couple. They are aware that the family is now resident in Northern Ireland.

The Trust had some challenges in determining parental responsibility as no documentation was provided by the carers and it took some time to receive confirmation of arrangement from Lithuanian authorities; delays were caused by the need to translate documents.

The arrangement is treated as private fostering in the UK. Meanwhile the carers also keep in touch with Lithuanian social services by telephone and email.

Language difficulties aside, it can be challenging for a UK-based practitioner to track down the parents or to verify what they have been told. For example, in order to protect the child's immigration status, information about the parents' whereabouts may be withheld from social workers. For example, a child who claimed asylum on grounds of political persecution, and stated that his parents were in hiding, is unlikely to pass on their contact details to an official, for fear of deportation. In addition to locating and retaining contact with parents overseas, it can be equally challenging for private fostering practitioners to keep track of the children themselves. Aside from situations in which children are being deliberately hidden from the authorities, the normality of private fostering in some cultures means that children may be passed on to other carers within the community, without any perceived need to update the parents, let alone the authorities.

Accessing services and support

Once a private fostering arrangement is confirmed, the local authority private fostering officer can play an important role in securing support and services for the child. This often involves the use of discretion, and occasional blurring of boundaries, in order to access financial or other resources. For example, we know of cases where English lessons designated for asylum seeking children have been provided for privately fostered children, thanks to the intervention of the private fostering officer. Section 17 monies (for children in need) can sometimes be accessed, for example if carers suddenly stop receiving financial support from parents.

Case 5.4: Kiran – an example of a child who entered the UK with a parent and was subsequently privately fostered

Kiran along with his father was sponsored by Kiran's cousin to come and reside with Kiran's cousin in Wales for a short time. Some time later, the cousin informed the police that Kiran's father had disappeared and the police notified children's services. The private fostering officer co-worked the case with a worker who had experience of casework with unaccompanied asylum seeking children.

An interpreter was used during the assessment process. The private fostering officer spoke with Kiran on his own, through the interpreter. Kiran stated that he was happy living with his cousin and that he did not wish to return to Bangladesh. He was not able to offer any explanation as to his father's whereabouts. Kiran's cousin explained that Kiran's brother had been asked if he could care for Kiran, but he refused as he did not want the responsibility. The police remained in contact during the assessment process, and also conducted additional checks on Kiran's cousin and his wife. These were found to be clear.

The assessment process did not reveal any areas of concern about the care that Kiran was receiving from his cousin. The private fostering officer liaised with Kiran's school to access additional support for Kiran via a voluntary service which works closely with schools in the area by supporting ethnic minority children with their education.

As Kiran was on a holiday visa the private fostering officer advised the cousin that if Kiran was residing with them, his immigration status would have to be secured. The private fostering officer advised also on the documentation and additional evidence that might support the application. Kiran has now been granted leave to remain in the UK.

The private fostering officer sought legal advice about Kiran's status with respect to private fostering, in particular whether it could be viewed that Kiran's father was consenting to the arrangement (as he knew who he was leaving Kiran with). It was necessary also to discuss the issue of parental responsibility for Kiran, as Kiran's father was missing and his mother is dead. The legal advice given was that Kiran's cousin should seek a Residence Order: an application for a Residence Order was made and an Interim Order granted, pending further assessment by the local authority. At this point the private fostering officer ceased to be involved with Kiran.

However, until his or her legal status is confirmed, it can be difficult to access services (e.g. health), particularly if immigration investigations are ongoing, and the child's documentation is held by the Home Office. Trafficked children may be forced to work, preventing them from accessing education: one private fostering officer described trying to track down some Turkish children known to be working in fast food outlets and whose address changed frequently, presumably to avoid private fostering assessment and associated investigations. Case 5.2 illustrates how Home Office and local authority expectations may differ as to whether a child is entitled to access education.

Attachment issues and longer-term planning

In private fostering arrangements, parental responsibility resides with the birth parent and, while reunification may be something that social workers would like to pursue, the private nature of the arrangement means that they have little influence over the course of events, other than to ensure that communication channels are kept open between the parents, carers and children involved. Compared to looked after children, where establishing permanency is a priority, for privately fostered children such a goal is far less tangible. For example, if there is a stated expectation that children will return to their parents at some future date, it would be inappropriate for the carer to apply for a Residence Order; such a situation may continue for years without resolution one way or the other and some children are effectively abandoned by their parents into private fostering arrangements, as in Cases 5.2 and 5.4.

Practitioners have particular concerns about children who are living away from their parents on a long-term basis. In some cases such arrangements started in infancy, potentially leading to insecure patterns of attachment and cultural dislocation. Schofield and Beek (2007) provide a thorough discussion of attachment issues in relation to children separated from their parents. It is not uncommon for arrangements to come to light that have been going on for many years. Although some studies (e.g. Owen *et al.* 2007) show that some private foster carers do provide good enough care, there are still concerns that others have little understanding of the loss and trauma and the cultural and racial issues that privately fostered children may face as a result of separation from their birth families, particularly if the arrangements last for any length of time. The situation where black children from abroad live in private fostering arrangements with white carers appears to be less prevalent than it was towards the end of the twentieth century, when concerns were raised both about the extent to which their cultural needs were being met in the UK, and how easy they would find it to be reunited with their birth family following a long stay in the UK. Private fostering practitioners in the rural counties where this was occurring report that the practice has declined. Practitioners suggest that privately fostered children sometimes receive inferior care to other children living in the same household, with just their basic physical needs being met and no attempt made to meet their emotional needs.

For newly arrived children, delays in decision making by the Home Office (plus further delays if appeals are made) can mean that any longer-term planning is left in limbo; this may in turn affect their attachments, possible reunification with their birth family, or plans to remain in the UK.

Leaving private fostering at age 16

Once unaccompanied migrant children living with distant relatives or unrelated adults turn 16, they are no longer deemed to be privately fostered and are liable to deportation, unless their immigration status is resolved and they are given leave to remain in the UK. Being left without any such legal protection is likely to have an adverse psychological impact on privately fostered children from abroad, who may already have faced much trauma in their lives. They now find themselves alone and unsupported with no one in the UK who has parental responsibility for them and no entitlement to reunification with their families or to the services of an independent legal guardian. They also lose the support of their private fostering social worker at this difficult time. Many find themselves in limbo as a result of their unregulated immigration status and go underground to avoid deportation. Anecdotal information from the Refugee Council and the BAAF Private Fostering Special Interest Groups suggest that many of these young people resort to substance misuse and prostitution in order to survive as they have no access to welfare services.

In contrast to children in public care, privately fostered children (except for privately fostered young people with a disability, children in need and those eligible under the Family and Friends Care Statutory Guidance for Local Authorities 2011, England) have no entitlement to support at their transition from care to independence. However, some local authorities do recognise their moral, if not legal, duty to support these vulnerable 16-year-olds by providing some kind of limited 'leaving care' service to privately fostered children.

Conclusion

The practice presented in this chapter suggests that more needs to be done to encourage professionals and the public to take a shared responsibility for identifying children in private fostering situations and notifying the local authority. For those separated children who fall outside of the other childcare classifications, the private fostering legislation provides a temporary – albeit minimal – safety net amidst the emotional turmoil and ongoing uncertainties of their immigration status, and offers a degree of support to children and their carers. However, the case examples also demonstrate the complexities involved in fulfilling the local authority's statutory duties, and the professional and cultural competencies required by private fostering officers to develop and maintain effective and trusting relationships both within their local communities and with a multitude of other professionals and agencies.

References

Association of Directors of Social Services (ADSS) (2005) *Response from the Association of Directors of Social Services to the DfES Consultation: 'Enhancement of the Private Fostering Notification Scheme'.* London: ADSS.

Department for Education and Skills (DfES) (2004) *The Every Child Matters, Change for Children Programme.* London: The Stationery Office.

Department of Health and Home Office (2003) *The Victoria Climbié Inquiry: Report of an inquiry by Lord Laming.* London: TSO.

Holman, B. (2002) *The Unknown Fostering: A Study of Private Fostering.* Lyme Regis: Russell House.

Macleod, M. (2010) *No Simple Answers: Report of the DCSF Advisory Group on Private Fostering.* London: DCSF.

Owen, C., Jackson, S., Barreau, S. and Peart, E. (2007) *An Exploratory Study of Private Fostering.* London: Institute of Education, Thomas Coram Research Unit.

Schofield, G. and Beek, M. (2007) *Attachment Handbook for Foster Care and Adoption.* London: BAAF.

Shaw, C., Brodie, I., Ellis, A., Graham, B. *et al.* (2010) *Research into Private Fostering.* London: DCSF.

Utting, W. (1997) *People Like Us: The Report of the Review of the Safeguards for Children Living Away From Home.* London: Department of Health and the Welsh Office.

Chapter Six

Safeguarding the Mental Health of Separated Children

Ruth Reed and Mina Fazel

Introduction

Children need to successfully negotiate a number of important developmental milestones in order to maximise their potential as adults. These milestones include physical, educational, cognitive, moral, emotional and behavioural goals. The stability of a child's home, school, family, friends and community provides the backdrop for optimal achievement at each step along these developmental trajectories. For any child, disruption in one of these arenas can have deleterious effects on psychological well-being and development. However, with appropriate support and the prompt reinstatement of stability after a change in circumstances, children rarely suffer significant longer-term adverse effects on their mental health.

All migrant children, whatever their ethnic, cultural, religious and linguistic background, face a considerable challenge in adapting to a new setting while also continuing their developmental progress towards adulthood. The majority of migrant children ultimately successfully negotiate potential obstacles and go on to higher education or employment and benefit from positive mental health. In contrast, separated migrant children not only are more likely to have suffered greater exposure to distressing events prior to arrival (Hodes *et al.* 2008), but also face the added difficulty of recovering from their experiences without the care and guidance of a parent, or even any substitute carer. For many, the struggle to make sense of past and present adversities is overwhelming in the absence of parental care, and separated children are therefore at considerable risk of psychological difficulties.

The term 'separated children' describes a variety of subgroups of children who may have very disparate experiences, ranging from materially advantaged children receiving a British education in a loving home, through to children entrapped for years in sexual servitude. One may reasonably question whether it makes sense to attempt to consider these children as a group in terms of the mental health consequences of their experiences. The reasons for so doing are, first, that the experience of separation from parents has long been recognised as almost universally distressing to varying degrees for pre-adolescent children, with even short separations having the potential for long-term disruptions to relationships, achievement and social development (Bowlby 1953). Very few children under the age of eight years would be expected to cope with a prolonged separation from their parents without distress, and the ability to cope with separation beyond this age is variable, depending upon the reasons and preparedness for separation, and the quality of substitute care provided. Second, separation from parents leaves children vulnerable to further adversity, particularly exploitation and abuse by substitute caregivers or other adults and children. Third, there is little choice in the case of 'invisible' groups (trafficked, undocumented migrant and some privately fostered children), where truly representative samples for research are unobtainable, other than to consider common experiences and their consequences for mental health based on studies of groups with similar experiences. Finally, there is a degree of crossover between subgroups of separated children, with trafficked adolescents sometimes being instructed to claim asylum, or unaccompanied asylum seeking children (UASC), whose asylum claim later fails, then remaining illegally in the UK. However, even within subgroups of 'separated children', there is great variation in the degree of exposure to distressing events and in the impact these events have on individual children, depending both on their pre-existing strengths and vulnerabilities, but also on their circumstances and support after such events.

In this chapter we first explore the range of psychological problems for which separated children are at particular risk, considering the factors which may promote resilience in the face of adversity, and those which may confer additional vulnerability. Thereafter, we discuss safeguarding concerns in two main arenas: identifying mental health problems, and accessing appropriate care for these problems. Untreated psychological problems in childhood and adolescence commonly persist into adult life and might therefore impact on the young person's functioning for many years, hence addressing this concern should be a high priority. The case examples provide a small glimpse into how services can develop in order to address these safeguarding concerns.

Mental health needs

Most common mental health problems

Separated children are not only vulnerable to the full range of mental health problems affecting children in general, but also at increased risk of certain disorders, particularly anxiety disorders, post-traumatic stress disorder (PTSD) and depression (Hossain *et al.* 2010) (see Box 6.1).

Box 6.1 – Common psychiatric disorders in separated children (World Health Organization 2007)

Anxiety disorders

A range of anxiety disorders may be seen in separated children, including generalised anxiety – present most of the time, with young people having a variety of fears and concerns. This can be accompanied by panic attacks that usually last for a few minutes and may have recognised triggers or occur 'out-of-the-blue'. The young person may greatly restrict his or her activities in order to avoid triggering an attack. Specific phobias may also arise in relation to past distressing experiences.

Post-traumatic Stress Disorder (PTSD)

PTSD can follow an extremely frightening or distressing event; the young person develops intrusive memories, flashbacks or nightmares relating to the event, and tries to avoid reminders of the event. A variety of other symptoms can be present including being constantly on edge, being irritable or angry, struggling to concentrate, feeling numb, an inability to recall aspects of the event, and sleep problems.

Depression

The three core symptoms of depression are low mood (or irritability in younger children), fatigue, and loss of interest in previously pleasurable activities. Additional symptoms include: sleep disturbance; low self-confidence; difficulty concentrating; decreased appetite; agitation; suicidal thoughts, with or without acts of self-harm; excessive feelings of guilt; hopelessness about the future; and feeling one can neither help oneself nor be helped. People with

---

depression may worry unduly about their health, or have physical symptoms without a clear medical cause; these presentations are more common in some cultures.

Self-harm

Deliberate self-harm is not a psychiatric disorder in itself; in many cases it is a behavioural manifestation of distress. It can be seen in those without any diagnosable psychiatric disorder, or can occur in the course of a psychiatric illness such as depression, PTSD, bipolar disorder, or psychosis. A minority of adolescents who repetitively self-harm will later go on to meet criteria for emotionally unstable personality disorder in adulthood; those who have been abused, particularly sexually abused, in childhood are more vulnerable to this outcome.

It is vital, however, to understand that although separated children may have a range of mental health symptoms, this does not equate in the majority of cases to their having a 'mental illness'. Some have suffered potentially traumatic events at the extremes of human experience. Although cumulatively the number of such distressing events is clearly linked to an increasing risk of psychological difficulty (Fazel *et al.* 2011), it is hard to be proscriptive about what constitutes a 'normal' or healthy psychological response to such exposures, and the range of typical responses within different cultures needs to be better understood. Some symptoms, such as flashbacks, are not inherently abnormal in those who have suffered very distressing experiences; they may be the mind's way of trying to process and recover from a traumatic memory (Brewin 2001). In determining whether a constellation of symptoms constitute a psychiatric disorder needing specialist treatment, it is the overall picture that is most useful – the frequency of symptoms, their nature, the level of distress they cause to the individual child, their progression over time, and their impact upon the child's ability to function in a healthy way within the family, school and peer settings.

Findings from studies on separated children

Most research on this group relates to adolescents rather than younger children; there is also a dearth of literature on the well-being of undocumented migrants and privately fostered children in the UK and other comparable countries. The research relating to asylum seeking and trafficked adolescents, though limited, is informative. As UASC are registered with children's services, they are a group more available to study, and studies have been carried out in the UK and other European countries, showing that UASC are at greater risk of psychological difficulties than accompanied asylum seeking children, migrants in general and the non-migrant population (Bean *et al.* 2007a; Derluyn, Broekaert and Schuyten 2008; Hodes *et al.* 2008). Approximately half suffer significant mental health problems, and these difficulties tend to persist in the medium term (Bean, Eurelings-Bontekoe and Spinhoven 2007b). They are at greater risk of anxiety, PTSD and depression, though they are less likely to show behavioural difficulties than the native population. Girls are more vulnerable than boys for developing mental health difficulties (Bean *et al.* 2007a). The effect of age on risk of mental health problems is unclear from the different studies (Fazel *et al.* 2011), but there is evidence that as UASC approach the age of 18 they have greater mental health difficulties (Bean *et al.* 2007a). This age-related deterioration is not seen in accompanied refugee children, and is believed to relate to the immigration determination procedure, when many fear deportation on reaching adulthood.

UASC differ from accompanied children in terms of their exposure to various risk factors for poor mental health, and have typically experienced more adverse events (Bean *et al.* 2007a; Derluyn, Mels and Broekaert 2009; Hodes *et al.* 2008). A study of UASC from 48 countries found that there were significant variations in risk depending upon the country of origin (Bean *et al.* 2007b). This could reflect differing responses to distressing events as well as differences in the nature of pre-migration traumatic events. Bullying, peer violence and discrimination are common adverse experiences after migration, and have negative effects on mental health (Almqvist and Broberg 1999; Ellis *et al.* 2008; Montgomery 2008; Sujoldzic *et al.* 2006). Further adverse events in their new countries can limit their ability to recover from previous distressing experiences, or occasionally lead to the development of psychiatric conditions in those who were free of symptoms on arrival (Montgomery 2008).

Some factors can reduce the risk of poor mental health. Resilient outcomes in terms of health and personal achievement are certainly not uncommon, though at present we have a limited understanding of the factors contributing to the maintenance or recovery of positive mental health (Reed *et al.* 2011). There appears to be a protective effect of placing UASC in care settings with at least one other child or adult caregiver of the same ethnic origin, and in facilitating contact with same-ethnicity peers (Geltman *et al.* 2005; Porte and Torney-Purta 1987). There is good evidence that having peers of any origin to socialise with and perceived support from peers is associated with fewer psychological difficulties (Almqvist and Broberg 1999; Berthold 1999). School and community integration are other important factors in improving mental health outcomes for asylum seeking children (Kia-Keating and Ellis 2007; Sujoldzic *et al.* 2006), and are of particular importance for UASC. Changes of school (Bean *et al.* 2007a; Montgomery 2008) and home (Bean *et al.* 2007b; Nielsen *et al.* 2008) can cause deteriorations in refugees' mental health and should be avoided if at all possible, whereas stability of education or employment is associated with positive outcomes (Montgomery 2008).

Trafficked, undocumented migrant and some privately fostered children come from 'invisible' populations and for ethical reasons cannot be studied in the environments in which they are living, such that any form of systematic study of their mental health *in situ* has not been achieved. Little research has been carried out to date on trafficked children (International Organization for Migration 2009). A valuable study conducted by Hossain *et al.* (2010) investigated women and girls accessing post-trafficking services in various European locations. About 12 per cent of the sample were under 18 and none was younger than 15, yet in the absence of child-specific studies, their findings are of interest. The women and girls scored highly for symptoms of anxiety and depression, and three-quarters had probable PTSD. The majority had experienced sexual and physical violence, threat, restriction of freedom and serious physical injury during their trafficking experience. High levels of anxiety and depressive symptoms were twice as common among those who had spent more than six months in a trafficked situation. Of note, a high proportion had also experienced abuse prior to being trafficked, highlighting the fact that the pre-migration experiences of this group are an additional source of adversity.

A Nepal-based study (Tsutsumi *et al.* 2008) investigated 164 returned adolescent girls and women formerly trafficked for sex work and other forms of exploitation. Almost all suffered from high levels of anxiety, and the majority also suffered depressive symptoms. One-third of those trafficked for sexual exploitation screened positive for PTSD. Of note, the average age of trafficking for non-sexual work was 11 and for sexual purposes was 16. The study illustrates the difficulty in trying to form trusting relationships when helping these women, as family members had initiated the process of trafficking in around a quarter of cases. This study also highlighted the lack of information available on how best to treat this group.

Separated, undocumented migrant children are universally disadvantaged and, like trafficked children, have a great number of risk factors for poor mental health. They are typically older adolescents exposed to considerable adversity prior to migration, coming either from socio-economically deprived backgrounds, and/or chaotic family circumstances. They have often experienced long, perilous migration journeys and may have had to use people traffickers to enter the UK. They may have experienced potentially traumatic events or abuse before, during or after their migration to the UK. Once in the UK, they are vulnerable to exploitation and abuse, and need to either work illegally – typically long hours in unregulated, unsuitable environments – or engage in begging, prostitution or criminal activity to survive. Not only are they exposed to multiple stressors, but also they have none of the buffers which can promote positive outcomes in adversity – school, family or stable peer relationships – and live in fear of discovery by the authorities, which prevents them seeking help if they are maltreated or physically or mentally unwell. Anxiety, PTSD and depression are again relatively common in this group, although reliable estimates of their prevalence are not obtainable, as they typically present to services only in emergencies such as suicidal crises.

In relation to privately fostered children, there is considerable variability in their pre-migration and post-migration circumstances. Many will be at little additional risk of mental health difficulties compared to the general migrant population, but even those in optimal circumstances still have the dual challenge of integrating into a different social, cultural and linguistic environment, and coping without their parents. For many, these will be surmountable hurdles, but for others who have different temperaments, social or academic skills, the degree of challenge may be too great and psychological distress might result. The more vulnerable might come from two groups. First, there are children who have involuntarily entered into private fostering arrangements due to difficulties in their home of origin, for example, the death of a parent; however good the foster home, the children are likely to experience problems coping with the dual burden of the original family stressor and an international transition. Second, there are children who, however good their childhood situation, are placed in an abusive home in the UK, and who are unable to voice their distress or are not listened to when they attempt to seek help from their family back home or from authority figures in the UK. Undue pressure to achieve beyond the child's capabilities can become emotionally abusive or lead to physical punishment, and may emanate from the host or home family. Such pressure to achieve may be common given the considerable expense involved for many families from low-income countries to set up such arrangements. The foster carers may simply see themselves as providing 'bed and board' and fail to acknowledge the child's need to be parented. Figure 6.1 shows some of the factors minimising psychological risk for this group.

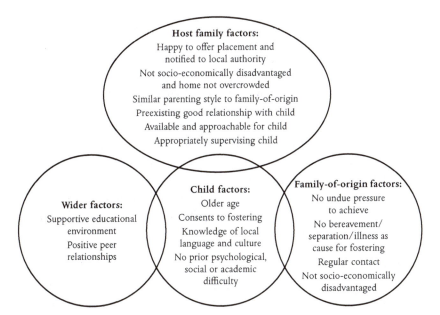

Figure 6.1: Factors minimising the risk of mental health difficulties for privately fostered children

The information available on pre-adolescent separated children (of whom there are relatively few) is more anecdotal than systematically collected. Anxieties and fears are common, and may be either unfocused or associated with a particular situation or object related to the traumatic experience. Such anxieties can disturb sleep through nightmares, bedwetting, frequent awakening, and cause difficulties in participation in age-appropriate activities and education. Children often re-enact frightening experiences through play or creative work. This may seem disturbing to those around them but is often a vital way for a child with limited language to make sense of traumatic memories. Outside of a specialist context, such play should neither be actively discouraged (beyond distraction to other activities) nor encouraged, providing that there is no risk of injury to the child or others. If such play is aggressive, risky, persistent over time, repetitive or preventing the child engaging in other activities, then specialist advice might be needed.

Safeguarding mental health

A number of important areas need to be addressed in order to safeguard the mental health needs of separated children. These children are particularly vulnerable and so awareness of these issues is of vital importance. In this chapter, the concerns are separated into the identification of mental health problems and then the appropriate management of those problems, including special circumstances to consider. Many of the issues are common to both identification and management, but are described only once.

Identification of mental health problems

A number of important barriers need to be addressed in order for the mental health needs of this group to be identified in the first instance, both in terms of non-mental health professionals facilitating referral, and in ensuring that children's needs are correctly identified once they have been referred to a mental health service.

ACCESS TO SERVICES

Many separated children are hidden from services, and the traditional referral routes might not be most appropriate to facilitate their access to professionals. Separated children need to know about the existence of services, what these services might do for them, and how to then access them. Migrants in general are more likely to access psychiatric care through emergency routes (Lindert et al. 2008), due to factors including stigmatisation of mental illness within their community, lack of knowledge of the health system and language barriers. Children without the legal right of entry into the UK may find it almost impossible to access healthcare. They may be actively prevented from seeking medical assistance if they are in forced labour in private homes or businesses, or may have no or limited knowledge of how the health system might work. Even those who are not deliberately restricted by others are likely to be fearful of discovery of their status and so reluctant to access healthcare, as has been shown among undocumented migrants in the USA (Berk and Schur 2001). As a result, trafficked and undocumented migrant children rarely present to mainstream healthcare services, unless in crisis. In such circumstances, they may voluntarily or under coercion use a false identity, particularly purporting to be of adult age, and a minder may closely supervise any contact with a health professional. On occasion, trafficked young people may be 'abandoned' if serious enough circumstances arise such that they need to seek urgent healthcare (such as late stage pregnancy), but due to fear and uncertainty, they may still not disclose their situation during contact with services. Health professionals should be alert to the possibility that a young person is a victim of trafficking in circumstances where the given age does not tally with appearance, where there is unusual reluctance to give standard information such as an address or to discuss social circumstances, or where the young person is under the constant supervision of an adult with whom they do not appear comfortable (Barrows and Finger 2008).

COMMUNICATION

The need to communicate properly is essential for the identification of mental health problems and their subsequent management. Effective communication requires overcoming linguistic and cultural barriers, alongside the building of trust to enable the child to feel it is safe to share information. The availability of good interpretation services is paramount, but moreover, professionals must have some appreciation of the pitfalls of using interpreters and how to overcome them – ideally though training or discussion with those who frequently use such services. The perspective of children as to whether they are comfortable with and trust the interpreter is essential, and they may benefit from hearing that the interpreter is also bound by patient confidentiality. Consistency of interpreter in assessment and subsequent contact helps in such sensitive work.

TRUST

It is often difficult for separated children to know whom they can trust and whether it is safe to share information about their past. In the absence of parents, separated children may have to relate to an extraordinary number of adults in caregiving roles of various forms. Not only can this be confusing, disempowering and counterproductive for children as they seek to establish new attachments, but also it can equally confound and paralyse the efforts of the adults to provide consistent care and engender a sense of security in children. In addition, unlike many children within the care system, whose personal and family history and previous contact with services might be well documented, little is known about the background of these children and therefore the assessor must rely almost entirely upon information that the children themselves provide. Disclosure of previous abuse or difficult early family experiences may not be easily shared, yet these issues are essential in understanding the presentation and subsequent management of a child. Similarly, information about past risky behaviours, including self-harm or violence towards others, will be known only if the child chooses to share them, which can make risk assessment challenging.

The sense of shame and stigma among those who have been victims of sexual abuse may be a considerable hurdle in accessing and accepting psychological intervention. Fear of disclosure to the community of origin may be particularly prominent among certain cultural groups, as girls can face ostracism and be considered unsuitable for marriage if they have been sexually active, irrespective of whether sexual experiences were consensual. It is vital to explain confidentiality, and the few conditions under which it might need to be broken, in a manner that the young person can understand. Difficulties establishing trust require that a small number of key, consistent and accessible individuals should work with an individual child, with whom a trusting relationship can develop over time.

Management of mental health problems

Once a potential problem has been identified, the considerable challenge of trying to help the separated child needs to be addressed. From a safeguarding perspective and also, importantly, considering the human rights of these children, it is essential to provide a treatment option that children trust, that is accessible and meets their needs. Ideally, the treatment would be based upon a clear evidence base for effectiveness, but unfortunately, even for relatively large populations such as refugees, there is presently a poor evidence base regarding best interventions (Murray, Davidson and Schweitzer 2010). Services that have been tailored for specific cultural groups and delivered in people's original languages are the most effective, but generally such services cannot be developed, given the heterogeneity of separated children accessing most services. Good practice examples include intervening early when needed, basing mental health treatments on best available evidence, good information-sharing between agencies and persistence in trying to engage separated children. Of note, there is support from the voluntary sector to facilitate contact between children and their families across international borders, including children who have been trafficked or who have sought asylum, notably Children and Families Across Borders (www.cfab.uk.net).

CULTURALLY SENSITIVE CARE

An ability to work in a culturally sensitive manner is key. The backgrounds of separated children are extremely diverse, but in order to provide culturally sensitive care for mental health difficulties, it is neither essential nor possible to have an understanding of all cultures; instead, an open-minded and non-judgemental approach alongside an exploration of the following elements facilitates care tailored to the needs of individual children:

- The children's perception of illness, and the cultural and spiritual dimensions which are relevant in their view of their physical and mental health symptoms.

- The wider context in which they view their experiences, and how they construct a sense of meaning from the difficulties they have faced, and continue to face.

- How their experiences impact on their sense of identity and how they feel others from their culture of origin and the local community view them, exploring any particular sense of shame or discrimination they may face.

- Their expectations of mental health services (International Organization for Migration 2009).

Therapeutic services with specialist experience of caring for trafficked or undocumented migrant children are few and far between. They are also difficult to plan as by their very nature, it is difficult to predict who might come, from where and what their needs might be.

INTERAGENCY WORKING

Separated children particularly benefit from good interagency communication and coordination. Mental health professionals need to have as much information as possible about a child's short-term and longer-term prospects for stability of carers, school and ultimately residency in the UK, in order to tailor the length and nature of an intervention to the child's needs. In return, they may help other involved professionals understand the manifestations of a child's distress and highlight ways in which those caring for the child in the school and home context can build upon the child's strengths and help the child find a variety of coping strategies to work through difficult emotions. It is also important that mental health professionals help other agencies to understand how to work constructively with challenging behaviours such as self-harm, substance misuse, inappropriate behaviours or aggression.

THERAPEUTIC APPROACHES

Both physical and legal safety are important prerequisites for the optimal delivery of therapy (Yakushko 2009), and mental health professionals need to work effectively with other involved professionals to ascertain the degree to which safety can be achieved prior to commencing treatment. Many children may, however, need to receive therapeutic intervention despite ongoing uncertainty. This situation can be therapeutically frustrating for both the therapist and the child, as a 'sticking plaster' approach to a deep-seated complex difficulty, but this is not to deny the necessity of such intervention being available nor that the relief of even some symptoms of distress can greatly improve a child's functioning, achievement and quality of life, even though he or she may have substantial ongoing difficulties which one cannot realistically hope to ameliorate in the midst of such precarious life circumstances. Group approaches to therapy in various forms can be helpful for refugee and migrant children in general, but may be unsuitable for trafficked children who can find it extremely difficult to trust not only therapists but also other young people (Yakushko 2009). Arts-based therapies such as music, dance, psychodrama and art have been used to transcend cultural and linguistic differences that can challenge the successful delivery of 'talking therapies' (Harris 2007; Koch and Weidinger-von der Recke 2009).

WORKING TOWARDS RECOVERY
Successful therapeutic work with children who have suffered highly distressing events is typically a long process requiring commitment from the child and therapist to achieve positive change. Therapeutic intervention requires, first, the re-establishment of a sense of security; second, to the extent which the child feels able and willing, addressing the symptoms and experiences which contributed to, or continue to contribute to, the child's distress; and finally, finding positive directions for the future, including establishing supportive and enduring relationships outside of the therapeutic setting, and integrating into age-appropriate peer activities, education, training or employment (International Organization for Migration 2009).

The process of recovery may involve frequent exacerbations of distress and relapse of symptoms, precipitated by external events or changes in children's understanding and appraisal of the events and their current circumstances. As a separated child may, through changes of foster carer or residential setting, have few other consistent adult presences in his or her life, the ability of a therapist to remain engaged with a child throughout the process of recovery, to be available at the times expected by the child, and to listen without judging or criticising, are vital cornerstones in the child's arduous journey towards learning to trust again. Conversely, certain aspects of interactions with professionals, such as lateness, leave, or job changes, can have particularly adverse effects on separated children. Careful and sensitive planning to help children prepare for any changes, or open and honest communication when situations change unexpectedly, for example due to therapist illness, are essential for this group to avoid both the rupture of a fragile bond of trust and the overwhelming sense of rejection which may be particularly powerful for these children. However optimal the circumstances and however experienced the therapist, painful emotions can inevitably be aroused, and may be directed at the therapist or substitute carer, given the absence of the real targets of anger – the soldiers who burnt down the family home, or the father who failed to protect his child from assault. Dealing constructively with anger, often unconscious, towards absent parents may be particularly difficult; such anger may manifest through 'acting out' behaviours, such as self-harm, substance misuse or rebelliousness.

CHALLENGES TO DELIVERING EFFECTIVE TREATMENT

Various factors may impact differently on the likelihood of successful mental health interventions for the different groups of separated children. Those in local authority care may be at genuine risk of return to their previous harmful environment – UASC often face the prospect of return to the country of origin, which can render psychological treatment particularly challenging to achieve. There is evidence, as mentioned above, that UASC's mental health can deteriorate with the approach of 18, whereupon the majority lose their right to remain in the UK. If these children are then placed in immigration detention facilities, this experience is likely to significantly negatively impact upon their mental health (Lorek *et al.* 2009); girls (Reijneveld *et al.* 2005) and younger unaccompanied children (Sourander 1998) in particular seem to fare worse. By being placed in detention facilities, they typically lose contact with supporting professionals, as they can be placed, at short notice, far away from their original places of residence. It is important to keep in mind a number of further special considerations for UASC. In the UK, when separated children turn 17, their care in children's services moves from the more supported 'Looked After System' to one of minimal support until they are 21 years old. There are particular concerns around the health of failed asylum seekers remaining in the UK, as they are not entitled to start any 'new episodes of care' within non-emergency secondary health services.

Finally, any threat of removal or deportation to their countries of origin raise many significant safeguarding concerns about what might happen to these children on arrival back to the country they have previously been forced to flee. How they are supported and prepared to leave the UK, what the impact their return might have on their families of origin and how these families will treat them, their general safety when they return and how this will be monitored, all are at present poorly addressed arenas of significant concern to professionals working with these young people.

Practice examples

As mentioned in the sections above, good practice includes effective interagency working, third sector involvement, harnessing school and community support systems and respecting the perspective of the child involved.

Rapidly accessible specialist services for trafficked children

Case 6.1 highlights a number of important areas for safeguarding the mental health of trafficked children.

Case 6.1: Jenny – an example of a trafficked child presenting with deliberate self-harm

Jenny was a 16-year-old student from China who was quiet and withdrawn at school, often appearing tired. She did not make any friends and would always go straight home after school. Unexpectedly, she self-harmed once at school, but refused to talk to anyone about this episode; she declined follow-up and her host family did not come into school when invited. On the last day of term, she threatened to kill herself at school, telling a teacher that she refused to return home. She claimed she was being abused, having been brought to the UK to do housework and childcare. This revelation precipitated an immediate referral to social services, as her disclosure made it unsafe for her to return to her host family. The urgent response from mental health services, social services and her school ensured that she was supported in her many needs. These included close monitoring of her mental state, immediate placement in a safe house to avoid contact from anyone associated with the abusive host family, and close, regular communication between the agencies involved. This all required considerable time and resources, but enabled Jenny to be safely placed in a foster home and to start a new school the following term. She settled well there, and gradually was able to build trusting relationships with peers, school staff and the professionals involved in her care.

Close and careful case coordination was a key factor in the management of Jenny's case and the presence of a significant constant person was essential in mitigating any mental health risks, as has been noted elsewhere (Beiser 2009). Such presentations are not uncommon for trafficked children (Pearce, Hynes and Bovarnick 2009). Of note, a special service, the NSPCC

Child Trafficking Advice and Information Line, is available to support professionals and signpost them to local services to help trafficked children (www.nspcc.org.uk/ctail).

School-based services for unaccompanied asylum seekers

Setting up school-based mental health services have been a model of how to reach unaccompanied asylum seekers. A number of projects have developed across the UK using the school as a base for delivering mental health services rather than traditional community and hospital settings (Fazel, Doll and Stein 2009; Health Protection Agency and DoH 2010; O'Shea *et al.* 2000). Working closely with staff in schools helps to identify those at risk and enables the development of a trusting relationship with the mental health professionals as the teachers both mediate and support the psychological work. Barriers to accessing mental health services for this population are reduced through provision in schools. An example of how such a service works can be seen in Case 6.2.

Case 6.2: Moses – an example of a traumatised unaccompanied asylum seeking minor

Moses was a 16-year-old unaccompanied asylum seeker from Africa who, a few weeks after arriving in the UK, was placed in a school with a number of other unaccompanied minors. The school had good language support for the new students, but little integration between new and established students. Teachers met weekly with the school-based mental health service and raised concerns a few weeks after Moses' arrival that he seemed distressed and preoccupied. Following consultation, the mental health professionals advised on strategies to support Moses to settle in school and kept his case under review. He initially seemed to improve but was subsequently involved in a fight with another student, prompting formal referral to the service. On assessment, his mood was noticeably low and he struggled to talk about his experiences in his native country, where his father had been killed and he had been forced to flee. He initially engaged well with the therapist, attending weekly for six weeks. Moses then stopped attending sessions, but by this time his teachers had noticed he was more settled. A few months later, he became withdrawn again, and agreed to join a therapeutic group for unaccompanied minors, where difficulties and aspirations were shared in a supportive environment. Even though Moses was one of a small percentage of separated children who was granted refugee status, his problems did not resolve when this happened; he required ongoing support from mental health and other professionals for a substantial period of time thereafter.

Case 6.2 illustrates some important practice points. Moses was seen at school, a familiar environment for him, avoiding disrupting his lessons. Working within the school environment enabled close and regular sharing of information about Moses' case. His teachers felt supported and played a key role in identifying the times when he was experiencing more difficulties, while also assisting his engagement with the service. When Moses stopped attending sessions, the therapeutic service was able to maintain indirect contact with him through the school staff and re-engage with him when later needed.

In research interviews conducted with unaccompanied minors who had been seen by school-based mental health services, the students stated that they found the service based in schools more supportive, accessible and helpful and many doubted as to whether they would attend a service elsewhere. As one young person stated in an interview with one of us (MF): 'it is good to have it in school, if come to hospital it is scary, I don't know if I would go if it was in a hospital...no one likes hospital'.

Conclusions

Separated children are particularly vulnerable to a number of mental health difficulties arising from the combination of multiple adverse experiences and a lack of parental support to aid recovery. However, with a prompt, flexible, child-centred and culturally informed response from services working in concert, the serious risks posed to their psychological well-being can be reduced to give them the best possible chance of a positive future.

References

Almqvist, K. and Broberg, A.G. (1999) 'Mental health and social adjustment in young refugee children 3 1/2 years after their arrival in Sweden.' *Journal of the American Academy of Child and Adolescent Psychiatry 38*, 6, 723–730.

Barrows, J. and Finger, R. (2008) 'Human trafficking and the healthcare professional.' *Southern Medical Journal 101*, 5, 521–524.

Bean, T., Derluyn, I., Eurelings-Bontekoe, E., Broekaert, E. and Spinhoven, P. (2007a) 'Comparing psychological distress, traumatic stress reactions, and experiences of unaccompanied refugee minors with experiences of adolescents accompanied by parents.' *Journal of Nervous and Mental Disease 195*, 4, 288–297.

Bean, T.M., Eurelings-Bontekoe, E. and Spinhoven, P. (2007b) 'Course and predictors of mental health of unaccompanied refugee minors in the Netherlands: One year follow-up.' *Social Science and Medicine 64*, 6, 1204–1215.

Beiser, M. (2009) 'Resettling refugees and safeguarding their mental health: Lessons learned from the Canadian Refugee Resettlement Project.' *Transcultural Psychiatry 46*, 4, 539–583.

Berk, M. and Schur, C. (2001) 'The effect of fear on access to care among undocumented Latino immigrants.' *Journal of Immigrant Health 3*, 3,151–156.

Berthold, S.M. (1999) 'The effects of exposure to community violence on Khmer refugee adolescents.' *Journal of Traumatic Stress 12*, 3, 455–471.

Bowlby, J. (1953) *Child Care and the Growth of Love.* Tonbridge, Kent: Whitefriars Press.

Brewin, C.R. (2001) 'Memory processes in post-traumatic stress disorder.' *International Review of Psychiatry 13*, 3, 159–163.

Derluyn, I., Broekaert, E. and Schuyten, G. (2008) 'Emotional and behavioural problems in migrant adolescents in Belgium.' *European Child and Adolescent Psychiatry 17*, 1, 54–62.

Derluyn, I., Mels, C. and Broekaert, E. (2009) 'Mental health problems in separated refugee adolescents.' *Journal of Adolescent Health 44*, 3, 291–297.

Ellis, B.H., MacDonald, H.Z., Lincoln, A.K. and Cabral, H.J. (2008) 'Mental health of Somali adolescent refugees: The role of trauma, stress, and perceived discrimination.' *Journal of Consulting Clinical Psychology 76*, 2, 184–193.

Fazel, M., Doll, H. and Stein, A. (2009) 'A school-based mental health intervention for refugee children: An exploratory study.' *Clinical Child Psychology and Psychiatry 14*, 2, 297–309.

Fazel, M., Reed, R.V., Panter-Brick, C. and Stein, A. (2011) 'Mental health of displaced and refugee children resettled in high-income countries: risk and protective factors.' *Lancet* (10 August 2011); DOI:10.1016/S0140-6736(11)60051-2.

Geltman, P.L., Grant-Knight, W., Mehta, C., Lloyd-Travaglini, S. *et al.* (2005) 'The "lost boys of Sudan": Functional and behavioral health of unaccompanied refugee minors re-settled in the United States.' *Archives of Pediatrics and Adolescent Medicine 159*, 6, 585–591.

Harris, D.A. (2007) 'Dance/movement therapy approaches to fostering resilience and recovery among African adolescent torture survivors.' *Torture 17*, 2, 134–155.

Health Protection Agency and Department of Health (2010) *Understanding the Health Needs of Migrants in the South East Region. A Report by the South East Migrant Health Study Group on Behalf of the Department of Health.* London: Health Protection Agency.

Hodes, M., Jagdev, D., Chandra, H. and Cunniff, A. (2008) 'Risk and resilience for psychological distress amongst unaccompanied asylum seeking adolescents.' *Journal of Child Psychology and Psychiatry 49*, 7, 723–732.

Hossain, M., Zimmerman, C., Abas, M., Light, M. and Watts, C. (2010) 'The relationship of trauma to mental disorders among trafficked and sexually exploited girls and women.' *American Journal of Public Health 100*, 12, 2442–2449.

International Organization for Migration (2009) *Caring for Trafficked Persons: Guidance for Health Providers.* Geneva: International Organization for Migration.

Kia-Keating, M. and Ellis, B.H. (2007) 'Belonging and connection to school in resettlement: Young refugees, school belonging, and psychosocial adjustment.' *Clinical Child Psychology and Psychiatry 12*, 1, 29–43.

Koch, S.C. and Weidinger-von der Recke, B. (2009) 'Traumatised refugees: An integrated dance and verbal therapy approach.' *Arts in Psychotherapy 36*, 5, 289–296.

Lindert, J., Schouler-Ocak, M., Heinz, A. and Priebe, S. (2008) 'Mental health, health care utilisation of migrants in Europe.' *European Psychiatry 23*, (Supplement 1), 14–20.

Lorek, A., Ehntholt, K., Nesbitt, A., Wey, E. *et al.* (2009) 'The mental and physical health difficulties of children held within a British immigration detention center: A pilot study.' *Child Abuse and Neglect 33*, 9, 573–585.

Montgomery, E. (2008) 'Long-term effects of organized violence on young Middle Eastern refugees' mental health.' *Social Science and Medicine 67*, 10, 1596–1603.

Murray, K.E., Davidson, G.R. and Schweitzer, R.D. (2010) 'Review of refugee mental health interventions following resettlement: Best practices and recommendations.' *American Journal of Orthopsychiatry 80*, 4, 576–585.

Nielsen, S.S., Norredam, M., Christensen, H.L., Obel, C. and Krasnik, (2008) 'Mental health among children seeking asylum in Denmark – the effect of length of stay and number of relocations: A cross-sectional study.' *BMC Public Health 8*, 293. DOI: 10.1186/1471-2458-8-293.

O'Shea, B., Hodes, M., Down, G. and Bramley, J. (2000) 'A school-based mental health service for refugee children.' *Clinical Child Psychology and Psychiatry 5*, 2, 189–201.

Pearce, J., Hynes, P. and Bovarnick, S. (2009) *Breaking the Wall of Silence: Practitioners' Responses to Trafficked Children and Young People.* London: NSPCC.

Porte, Z. and Torney-Purta, J. (1987) 'Depression and academic achievement among Indochinese refugee unaccompanied minors in ethnic and nonethnic placements.' *American Journal of Orthopsychiatry 57*, 4, 536–547.

Reed, R.V., Fazel, M., Jones, L., Panter-Brick, C. and Stein, A. (2011) 'Mental health of displaced and refugee children resettled in low-income and middle-income countries: Risk and protective factors.' *Lancet* (10 August 2011); DOI:10.1016/S0140-6736(11)60050-0.

Reijneveld, S.A., de Boer, J.B., Bean, T. and Korfker, D.G. (2005) 'Unaccompanied adolescents seeking asylum: Poorer mental health under a restrictive reception.' *Journal of Nervous and Mental Disease 193*, 11, 759–761.

Sourander, A. (1998) 'Behavior problems and traumatic events of unaccompanied refugee minors.' *Child Abuse and Neglect 22*, 7, 719–727.

Sujoldźić, A., Peternel, L., Kulenović, T. and Terzić, R. (2006) 'Social determinants of health – a comparative study of Bosnian adolescents in different cultural contexts.' *Collegium Antropologicum 30*, 4, 703–711.

Tsutsumi, A., Izutsu, T., Poudyal, A.K., Kato, S. and Marui, E. (2008) 'Mental health of female survivors of human trafficking in Nepal.' *Social Science and Medicine 66*, 8, 1841–1847.

World Health Organization (2007) *The ICD-10 Classification of Mental and Behavioural Disorders: Clinical Descriptions and Diagnostic Guidelines (10th Revision).* Geneva: WHO.

Yakushko, O. (2009) 'Human trafficking: A review for mental health professionals.' *International Journal for the Advancement of Counselling 31*, 3, 158–167.

Acknowledgement

Thanks to C. Dodd for a helpful discussion in preparation of the chapter.

Chapter Seven

Return of Separated Children to Countries of Origin

Nadine Finch

Introduction

The prospect of being returned to their country of origin is possibly the single biggest cause of anxiety for separated children (Kohli 2006). Broadly speaking most young people face this issue as they turn 18, although the threat of removal and return is ever present from their point of arrival in the UK. Unaccompanied or separated children can be returned to their country of origin only if the Secretary of State is satisfied that adequate reception arrangements are in place for them there. However, even now there are exceptions where a child has previously claimed asylum in another EU country (Dublin II Regulation) or where he or she has erroneously been assessed to be an adult (Crawley 2007). For a number of years The Secretary of State for the Home Department has also been developing a policy for returning children prior to their 18th birthday to some countries of origin. This chapter explores the reasons why some children, and more specifically boys of 16 and 17 from Afghanistan, may be returned to their country of origin in the future.

Return to Afghanistan

In March 2010 a tender document was issued by the UK government. It invited bids for the provision of reintegration assistance in Kabul for 120 adult males and also up to 12 Afghan boys a month. A negligible number of unaccompanied or separated Afghan girls have arrived in the UK to date and claimed asylum and therefore they have not been included in these plans. There has as yet been no announcement about the identity of any contractor who may be awarded this contract. Press publicity suggested that the £4 million contract was for the construction of a reception centre in Kabul for unaccompanied or separated children (Travis 2010). However, non-governmental organisations (NGOs) now understand that the contractor will be expected to build a reintegration centre, which will cater for Afghan men whose applications for international protection has been refused in the UK. It is still not clear what provision is planned for boys and whether it will be in a centre or elsewhere (whether provision for the boys will be in that same centre or will be with adult supervisors). At the same time NGOs in Europe believe similar arrangements are being made in Norway, Sweden, Denmark and the Netherlands to return children to Afghanistan at the point at which they are refused international protection (UNHCR 2010b). For example, Denmark is reported to be planning to return unaccompanied minors to orphanages in Afghanistan (UNHCR 2010a, p.25). It would appear that Afghan unaccompanied or separated boys have been singled out because statistics show that a substantial proportion of unaccompanied or separated children arriving in Europe come from Afghanistan. The data produced by the UK Home Office support this general proposition but do not illuminate the Home Office's reasons for doing so.

Data from Norway suggest that there has been a rapid rise in the number of unaccompanied or separated children arriving from Afghanistan; only 89 arrived in 2007 but this rose to 1750 in 2009 (Boland 2010, p.63). However, a wider study by the UNHCR suggests that the motives for such children leaving Afghanistan are complex and mixed (Mougne 2010). The situation in the UK is somewhat different. The overall number of unaccompanied or separated children arriving in the UK has historically been high and can be correlated with wars, civil strife and insurgency in their countries of origin. In 1998, 3037 unaccompanied or separated children were documented as arriving in the UK; these figures have remained broadly consistent, apart from a notable surge in 2002, when 6007 arrived. (However, figures for 1998–2001 are known to be an underestimate as not all of the applications from these children were recorded.) In 2002, the number of unaccompanied or separated children from Afghanistan arriving in the UK was exceeded only by such children arriving from Iraq and the Federal Republic of Yugoslavia. In 2003, only numbers from Somalia were larger. Since 2004, Afghan boys have constituted the largest group of unaccompanied or separated minors arriving in the UK. The data in Table 7.1 indicates that children from Afghanistan continue to represent a substantial proportion of overall numbers for separated children in the UK.

Table 7.1 Arrivals of separated children from Afghanistan to the UK

Date	Total	Total from Afghanistan
2007	3645	984
2008	4285	1714
2009	3500	1750

Source: Home Office, Research, Development and Statistics Directorate – Control of Immigration: Statistics United Kingdom.

There have been a number of pieces of research, which have focused on the arrival of increasing numbers of unaccompanied or separated Afghan boys in Europe; statistics consistently reveal that Afghan girls do not arrive on their own in Europe in any significant numbers and the few that have been recorded have arrived with their brothers or other relatives (Mougne 2010). One report (Boland 2010) was initiated by governments of the UK and Norway. It contains much useful data about the dangers these children face on their journeys to Europe. Children described the journey as hazardous and said that they experienced cruel and inhumane treatment by smugglers as well as by some law enforcement officials. Families were given false promises about the level of care and conditions that the children would experience during the journey. Several children said they witnessed other children being beaten when they protested and left to die when they could not keep up with the group.

However, its conclusions need to be viewed with caution. In 2009, 1500 unaccompanied or separated children from Afghanistan arrived in the UK and 1750 arrived in Norway that year, and yet only 20 unaccompanied or separated children were interviewed for the purposes of this research. In addition, the adults who were interviewed in Afghanistan were not the parents of, or related to, the children interviewed. As a consequence any comparison between the reasons given by the children for their journey to Europe and the account given by the adults about sending sons to Europe is potentially misleading. The fact that 'families interviewed in Afghanistan who have a child in the west said that the decision was made because of the need to provide financial support and good economic prospects for their son' (Boland 2010, p.56) did not mean that when the 20 children interviewed in destination countries of UK and Norway who said that their journeys were made because their lives were in danger for a political or personal reason were lying.

The findings section of *Children on the Move* went on to assert that 'all the children said that existing levels of security, education and employment prospects open to them in Afghanistan were limited or non-existent' (Boland 2010, p.56) and concluded that 'until these needs are met, children and their families will make the decision to have a child on the move to a western country' (Boland 2010, p.56). However, as can be seen below, this was not the only reason children fled from Afghanistan.

Research conducted by the United Kingdom Border Agency (UKBA) for a project financed by the European Commission stated that the National Register for Unaccompanied Children (NRUC, a register which can be accessed by the UKBA and the local authorities accommodating unaccompanied and separated children) suggests that legislative restrictions placed on single adult asylum applicants and families introduced new incentives for adults to claim to be children and for families to present their children as unaccompanied (Rice and Poppleton 2009). However, this report did not provide any evidence or data to show that a significant number of unaccompanied or separated Afghan children fabricated their age or accounts of events which had happened to them in Afghanistan. At the same time objective evidence such as that referred to by the UKBA in its own *Country of Origin Information Report* on Afghanistan in 2008 indicated that 'the security situation in Afghanistan is assessed by most analysts as having deteriorated at a constant rate throughout 2007' (UKBA 2008, p.27).

In addition, a statement by a NATO spokesman that children were safer in Kabul than Glasgow attracted widespread criticism from NGOs working in the field in Afghanistan (Boone 2010). For example, the chief executive of Save the Children was quoted as saying: 'we should be listening to what children in Afghanistan are saying. Last year was the deadliest for children since late 2001, with more than a thousand killed because of the conflict' (Boone 2010).

A further UNCHR report adopts a more holistic view to the recent movement of unaccompanied or separated Afghan children (Mougne 2010). It noted that 'the number of young people involved in this movement remains very small in relation to the size of the Afghan population as a whole and in relation to the number of Afghan refugees and displaced people in the sub-region' (Mougne 2010, p.8). It also stated that 'in this complex context, the traditional notions of "refugee movement" and "economic migration" would appear to have very limited value, especially when employed in a binary manner' (Mougne 2010, p.8). As stated in the background paper presented to the 2007 High Commissioner's Dialogue on Protection Challenges:

> UNHCR recognizes that some of the people involved in mixed movements may also have mixed motivations. When a person decides to leave her or his own country and seek admission to another state, she or he may be prompted by a combination of fears, uncertainties, hopes and aspirations which can be difficult to unravel. This is particularly so when people are leaving countries that are simultaneously affected by human rights violations, armed conflict, ethnic discrimination, unemployment and deteriorating public services. (Mougne 2010, p.9)

Return to other countries

The recent UK proposals are specific to Afghan boys of 16 and 17 years but illustrate a far wider concern about the number of unaccompanied or separated children who are now said to be arriving in Europe to seek asylum.

The *Action Plan on Unaccompanied Minors (2010–2014)* agreed by the European Commission in 2010 acknowledged in its introduction that

> the reasons behind the arrival of this particularly vulnerable category of children are manifold: to escape from wars and conflicts, poverty or natural catastrophes, discrimination or persecution; to be sent by their family in the expectation of a better life or in order to access education and welfare, including medical attention; to join family members; as victims of trafficking destined for exploitation, etc. (European Commission 2010, p.2)

In the UK itself the change in attitude towards unaccompanied or separated children dates back many years and is not a result of the change of government. As early as 2003–2004 the previous Labour government was planning pilot return programmes. For example, in January 2005 the government announced that it would be returning children to Albania as part of a pilot programme for the return of unaccompanied or separated children to their countries of origin (UNICEF 2005). In March 2005 the Immigration and Nationality Directorate then issued an Unaccompanied Asylum Seeking Children Returns Programme, which indicated that the relevant local authority would be asked to produce an assessment of the unaccompanied or separated child's needs within 42 days and then it would be asked to meet with the Directorate to decide how any needs could best be met by a 'Match and Transfer' pathway to return.

The pilot programme never became operational due to indications from UNICEF and the Albanian coalition All Together Against Child Trafficking that they could not support the programme. The Albanian government also failed to agree to sign the necessary 'technical agreement' with the UK government. Therefore, the UKBA's policy remained that it would return unaccompanied or separated children to their country of origin only when it was satisfied that adequate reception and care arrangements were in place there. However, as the UKBA had no procedures in place to ascertain whether there were adequate reception and care arrangements in place, individual children were not generally returned to their countries of origin. Further pilot projects to Angola and Vietnam were explored but did not become operational due to a failure to identity suitable 'partners' in these countries of origin. The government and the UKBA remained committed to establishing such a returns procedure and more recently 'scoping exercises' were carried out in Bangladesh, Pakistan and Afghanistan.

An amended and updated returns policy was also published in a consultation paper, issued in February 2007. This focused on the availability of 'adequate reception arrangements', as opposed to 'adequate care and reception arrangements' and stated that the policy to grant discretionary leave to all unaccompanied or separated children who were refused asylum was to be reassessed. At paragraph 48 of this consultation paper the UK government stressed that it intended to promote 'voluntary return, to include relevant re-integration assistance in the country of origin' (Home Office 2007) but that 'if this offer of voluntary assistance is not accepted and integration into the UK is not an option, enforced return will be the norm' (Home Office 2007).

The consultation led to the publication of *Better Outcomes: The Way Forward. Improving the Care of Unaccompanied Asylum Seeking Children* (Home Office 2009). Its Key Reform Five was entitled *Resolving Immigration Status More Quickly and Enabling Care Planning to Focus on Integration or Early Return to the Country of Origin*. In paragraph 6.2 it states: 'where it is safe to do so and reception arrangements are in place, an unaccompanied asylum seeking child will be expected to return to his country of origin at the earliest opportunity once a decision is made and all appeal rights are exhausted'. The current policy can be found in paragraph 17.7 of *Processing an Asylum Application from a Child*, where it states:

> The UK Border Agency has a policy commitment that no unaccompanied child will be removed from the United Kingdom

unless the Secretary of State is satisfied that safe and adequate
reception arrangements are in place in the country to which the
child is to be removed. (Home Office 2010, p.45)

No explanation was given as to how the 'adequacy' of reception
arrangements was to be assessed but the information disclosed to date
suggested that reception arrangements are being designed to meet the
general needs of 16- or 17-year-old Afghan boys. It is likely that this
approach will be challenged in the courts. In the case of R (on the
application of A) v National Asylum Support Service and another [2003]
EWCA, a case involving accommodation provided to asylum seekers in the
UK, the Court of Appeal held that 'adequacy' was a concept that must be
defined in relation to the particular needs of the individual in question and
did not just have a general meaning.

It is also not clear whether the present returns policy will conform with
the European Union *Action Plan on Unaccompanied Minors*. A commitment
to develop such an Action Plan was included in the Five Year Strategy
on Asylum and Migration, which was part of the Stockholm Programme,
announced at the end of 2009. The Programme expressly asked the
European Commission to 'examine practical measures to facilitate the
return of the high number of unaccompanied minors that do not require
international protection' (European Commission 2010, p.2).

The European Commission held a number of consultation meetings and
then formulated a Communication from the Commission to the European
Parliament and the Council entitled an *Action Plan on Unaccompanied Minors
(2010–2014)*. In the introduction to the Plan the Commission asserted
that the common approach to be adopted by the European Union 'should
be based on the respect for the rights of the child as set out in the EU
Charter of Fundamental Rights and the United Nations Convention on the
Rights of the Child and in particular the principle that "the best interests
of the child"' (European Commission 2010, p.3) must be the primary
consideration in all action related to children taken by public authorities.

The Action Plan then continued in paragraph 5.1 to adopt a purposive
and child-centred approach to the question of returning unaccompanied or
separated children to their countries of origin by stating that:

It is likely that in many cases the best interest of the child is to
be reunited with his/her family and to grow up in his/her own
social and cultural environment...However, return is only one of
the options and the best interests of the child must always be a
primary consideration. Voluntary departure must be prioritised.
(European Commission 2010, p.12)

Directive 2008/115/EC on the Common Standards and Procedures in Member States for Returning Illegally Staying Third Country Nationals also addresses the issue of returning and removing unaccompanied minors (European Union 2000). The UK has not opted into this directive but its contents represent an accepted interpretation of the international law applicable to these children. Article 10 of the directive states that:

1. Before deciding to issue a return decision in respect of an unaccompanied minor, assistance by appropriate bodies other than the authorities enforcing return shall be granted with due consideration being given to the best interests of the child.

2. Before removing an unaccompanied minor from the territory of a Member State, the authorities of that Member State shall be satisfied that he or she will be returned to a member of his or her family, a nominated guardian or adequate reception facilities in the State of return. (European Commission 2008)

Even though the UK has not opted into this directive, it attends contact meetings about the directive and works with other Member States on issues arising from the directive. At a meeting of the Contact Committee in 2010 a number of concerns were raised by NGOs about the implementation of Article 10.2, because it appears to assume that returning an unaccompanied or separated child to his or her family will be a safe and sustainable solution.

Neither Article 3 of the directive nor the UK's returns policy provides a definition of the family members being referred to. This could potentially expose a child to exploitation and abuse. Those working in the immigration and asylum field will be aware that in many societies there is a very loose use of the term 'uncle', 'aunt' or 'brother' and the child may not have knowledge of their exact relationship to a 'relative'. These children are also unlikely to have reliable identity cards or passports in their possession as they will have fled from persecution or been smuggled by agents under false identities. In addition, the lack of a reliable birth certificate system and the high rates of illiteracy in some countries or communities means that it can be difficult to verify a child's identity through official sources. This means that a number of children may be left in the care of adults to whom they are not related and who have no parental responsibility for them.

Article 10.2 also refers to the authorities of a Member State being 'satisfied' that the child will be returning to family members and this implies a high test of certainty, with the burden of proof falling on the Member State wishing to return a child to a country of origin. It would not be sufficient for the authorities to conclude that it was reasonably likely that they were related as claimed. The need to adopt a higher test of 'satisfaction' was accepted by the Secretary of State for the Home Department in AA (Afghanistan) v Secretary of State for the Home Department [2007] EWCA, a case involving the return of a minor to Afghanistan. In that case the Secretary of State had argued that his return to Kabul could be justified by the fact that he had said that he had once lived there with an uncle for six months. The Court of Appeal disagreed and found that enquiries had to be made before it could be said that adequate reception arrangements were still in place there.

In the UK document, *Better Outcomes: The Way Forward. Improving the Care of Unaccompanied Asylum Seeking Children*, the Home Office asserted that 'as a general rule the needs of children are best served by being with their families' (Home Office 2009, p.12). This may well be the case where the family structure is one which nurtures minor children and where the parents aspire to provide their children with the advantages and protections which they experienced as children or would have liked to experience. Unfortunately, this model is not universal. As practitioners are aware, in some societies children are viewed as merely part of the family's potential wealth and it would be socially acceptable to 'sell' a girl into an under-age marriage or to a human trafficker if that would benefit the wider family. In other communities and societies the actions of children are judged harshly against ideals dedicated to protecting the reputation and 'honour' of the family. In extreme cases children may be viewed as the cause of a family's misfortune and be deemed to be 'witches' or 'demons' (DCSF 2007, p.6) or killed as they have damaged the family's 'honour' by being raped and prostituted (UKBA 2008, p.5)

As a consequence successful 'family tracing' is not sufficient to ensure a durable solution for unaccompanied or separated children. A safe return mechanism can be achieved only if the viability of returning a child to a family or relative is assessed both in terms of the family's ability to support and nurture that child and also its ability to protect the child from further possible exploitation. This assessment process would require a home visit to check the authenticity of any claims being made by the adults. It would also be important to ascertain whether the family acknowledges that children also have rights as defined in the UN Convention on the Rights of the Child, which may at times be in conflict with the rights being asserted by adult members of the family. In addition, it would be important to recall that the UNCRC assumes that a child's views will also be taken into account.

Such viability assessments would best be carried out by childcare professionals who are both aware of the international standards, which now prevail as best practice, and also have experience in assessing family dynamics, strengths and weaknesses. The areas to be explored would be the family's socio-economic situation, the proposed care arrangements and the safety and security of the placement as suggested in paragraph 84 of Committee on the Rights of the Child's General Comment No. 6 (UNCROC 2005). It will also be necessary to undertake such assessments before a child actually returns to a country of origin in the light of the likely paucity of social welfare 'safety nets' in such countries and the likelihood that there would not be institutions which would have a duty to intervene if child protection concerns arose at a later date. In many countries of origin there will be no functioning social services infrastructure and no NGOs which fulfil a similar role.

One further important consideration is whether those given the responsibility for deciding to return an unaccompanied or separated child to a country of origin have any possible 'vested interest' in the decision. Both the UKBA and children's services departments have a financial interest in divesting themselves of responsibility for these children. The need to ensure that an assessment is impartial has been recognised in the *UNHCR Guidelines on Determining the Best Interests of the Child* (UNHCR 2008), where it recommended that no one body should decide on which solution would be in a child's best interests and that the decision should be made by a panel of disinterested individuals.

At the Contact Committee on the Returns Directive mentioned above one of the major concerns of a number of Member States was whether the arrangements made for the reception of unaccompanied or separated children were durable and whether there was a body who would assist the children if the arrangements did not turn out to be sustainable.

Article 3 of the UNCRC does not assert that the best interests of the child must necessarily be the paramount consideration. However, jurisprudence in the UK is increasingly acknowledging the importance of the best interests principle. This culminated in the Supreme Court decision in ZH (Tanzania) v Secretary of State for the Home Department [2011] UKSC 4, where it was held that when considering this principle the most relevant national and international obligation of the UK is contained in Article 3(1) of the UNCRC (UK Supreme Court 2011, para. 23). Lady Hale also went on to hold that the best interests of a child must be the first consideration (UK Supreme Court 2011, para. 26). The Supreme Court also quelled any remaining doubts about the applicability of the UNCRC by finding that

> article 3 was a binding obligation in international law, and [that] the spirit, if not the precise language, had been translated into our national law. [As] section 11 of the Children Act 2004 places a duty upon a wide range of public bodies to carry out their

functions having regard to the need to safeguard and promote the welfare of children. (p.12)

There is also a long line of case law in the higher courts which confirm that when a court is taking into account the provisions of the ECHR, which has largely been incorporated into UK domestic law in the Human Rights Act 1998, it can use other international conventions when considering the proper application of provisions in the European Convention. For example, in ID and Others v Home Office, which involved the detention of families with children in Yarls Wood Immigration Removal Centre, the Court of Appeal reminded itself that it could take into account the provisions in Article 38 of the UNCRC when considering whether there had been a breach of Article 8 of the European Convention on Human Rights.

However, the difficulty remains that in domestic family and immigration law, there is no definition of the phrase 'the best interests of the child'. In relation to returns policy, this gap can be filled in part by the guidance provided by the United Nations Committee on the Rights of the Child in paragraph 84 of its General Comment No. 6 on *Treatment of Unaccompanied and Separated Children Outside Their Country of Origin*, which states that:

> Return to the country of origin shall in principle only be arranged if such return is in the best interests of the child. Such a determination shall, inter alia, take into account:

- The safety, security and other conditions, including socio-economic conditions, awaiting the child upon return, including through home study, where appropriate, conducted by social network organizations;

- The availability of care arrangements for that particular child;

- The views of the child expressed in exercise of his or her right to do so under Article 12 and those of caretakers;

- The child's level of integration in the host country and the duration of absence from the home country;

- The child's right to preserve his or her identity, including nationality, name and family relations;

- The desirability of continuity in a child's upbringing and to the child's ethnic, religious, cultural and linguistic background. (UNCRC 2005, para. 84)

The Committee and Article 12 of the UNCRC require a State Party to take into account the views of the child who is to be returned. There would not appear to be any mechanism for this to happen in the present UK plans to return unaccompanied or separated children to their countries of origin. In fact, when previous pilot return programmes were discussed the children were not to be alerted in case this caused them to abscond from their local authority accommodation and put themselves at risk on the street. A number of NGOs working with this group of children have also expressed concerns as to whether a minor can give informed consent to being returned without a legal guardian acting on his or her behalf. Certainly if a judicial review is brought against any such decision to return him or her, he or she will have to obtain a litigation friend in order to bring such a claim as children are not deemed competent to give undertakings in these or other court proceedings.

In its most recent report into the UK's compliance with the UNCRC, the UN Committee on the Rights of the Child expressed its concern that 'there is no independent oversight mechanism, such as a guardianship system, for an assessment of reception conditions for unaccompanied children who have to be returned' (UNCRC 2008, paras. 70 and 71). It then went on to recommend that the UK should consider the appointment of guardians for separated children and 'ensure that when the return of children occurs, this happens with adequate safeguards, including an independent assessment of the conditions on return' (UNCRC 2008, paras. 70 and 71).

A similar position has also been adopted in the European Union's (2010) *Action Plan on Unaccompanied Minors (2010–2014)*, where it is stressed that:

> Assistance to minors should be a continuous and stable process, which should include the return and post-return phase. In all cases, the return must be conducted in a safe, child-appropriate and gender-sensitive manner. The challenges in this respect are to ensure that the minors are returned in full respect of international standards and that they will be accepted in their home environment. Work on the ground is fundamental in convincing families and communities to welcome the minor's return, as well as to prevent stigmatisation and further victimisation in cases of trafficking in human beings. ...Reintegration should also be monitored to ensure that no major problems arise. (European Commission 2010, para. 5.1)

Return to other EU countries

Other considerations apply when the UK is considering removing an unaccompanied or separated asylum seeking child to another country within the European Union. These arise from the provisions of the Dublin II Regulation, which state at Article 6:

> Where the applicant for asylum is an unaccompanied minor, the Member State responsible for examining the application shall be that where a member of his or her family is legally present, provided that this is in the best interests of the minor. In the absence of a family member, the Member State responsible for examining the application shall be that where the minor has lodged his or her application. (European Commission 2003, Article 6)

Where the unaccompanied or separated child has relatives in another Member State, the Regulations properly ensure that a child will be returned to that family member's care only if it is in his or her best interests. In contrast to proposals to return children to non-EU states there is no suggestion that his or her best interests are only one of a number of primary factors to be taken into account. Therefore the test concentrates on the particular needs and interests of that individual child.

Article 2 of the Regulations defines exactly who will be viewed as a family member of an unaccompanied minor and states that it will be his or her father, mother or guardian as long as they formed a family in his or her country of origin. It also states that the fact that the child was born to an unmarried parent does not prevent him or her from relying on the relationship. This is a narrow definition but it does protect unaccompanied or separated children from being returned to someone who is either not related to them at all or is at best very distantly related to them. Given the high incidence of unaccompanied or separated children being subjected to exploitation and human trafficking by adults, some of whom may be related to them, this is an important provision.

The implementation of a strict 'best interests' test should also ensure that an unaccompanied or separated child is not returned to a parent or guardian who may abuse or exploit him or her. However, when an unaccompanied or separated child is not being returned to join a family member but is being returned as he or she previously made an application for asylum in another Member State, there is no explicit reference to ensuring that a child is not returned unless it is in his or her best interests.

Nevertheless, when reaching a decision to return an unaccompanied or separated child to another Member State the Secretary of State for the Home Department will have to comply with the duty which arises under Section 55 of the Borders, Citizenship and Immigration Act 2009. This requires her to have regard to the need to safeguard and promote the welfare of children who are in the UK when discharging any immigration function (see Case 7.1). In the case of R (on the application of TS) v The Secretary of State for the Home Department [2010] EWHC, Mr Justice Wyn Williams held at paragraph 25 that this 'duty arose not just in relation to the process of removal but also in relation to whether or not removal should be directed'.

Case 7.1: Farzam's experiences of the Dublin II Regulation

Tahir was an unaccompanied asylum seeker child from Afghanistan who had applied for asylum in Belgium on 7 November 2008. He had then travelled on to the UK, where he claimed asylum on 15 January 2009. A County Council accepted that he was a minor and accommodated him. When his fingerprints were matched with those taken in Belgium, it was asked to accept him back. Tahir asserted that he should not be returned there as he was now settled in the UK and was attending school. On 26 October 2010 the High Court held that the Secretary of State for the Home Department had not shown that she had complied with Section 55 of the Borders, Citizenship and Immigration Act 2009 and had regard to the need to safeguard and promote his welfare when deciding to return him to Belgium. In particular it found that the Secretary of State had not taken into account the fact that there was medical evidence which indicated that his removal to Belgium would exacerbate his post-traumatic stress disorder. Therefore the Secretary of State had to review her decision, taking all his circumstances into account.

Children who have been victims of human trafficking

The UK ratified the Council of Europe's Convention on Action against Trafficking in Human Beings in 2008 and it came into force in the UK on 1 April 2009. Article 16 states that 'child victims [of trafficking] shall not be returned to a State, if there is indication, following a risk and security assessment, that such return would not be in the best interests of the child'. Therefore when the Secretary of State for the Home Department is considering returning a child who was a victim of trafficking in the past, she has to apply a more stringent test than that applied to other unaccompanied or separated children who are being returned to countries of origin. Article 3 of the UNCRC obliges the Secretary of State for the Home Department to remind herself that when deciding whether to return a child his or her their best interests must be a primary consideration and following ZH (Tanzania), his or her best interests would also have to be considered first. When returning a trafficked child her concentration has to be on whether it is in 'the' best interests of the child to be returned. This could be interpreted as meaning that their best interests would be a determinative factor not just a first consideration. However, there is as yet no case law on this point and no practice has been established as most unaccompanied children, who have been trafficked and who come to the attention of the UKBA, claim asylum and are not under present policy removed to countries of origin while they are still minors, even if their applications for asylum are refused. Similarly, Article 10.4c of the Convention on Action against Trafficking in Human Beings states that efforts to locate a child's family should be made only when this is in the best interests of the child.

Conclusion

At present unaccompanied or separated children whose applications for asylum or other international protection are refused are not removed to countries of origin while they are still minors. They may be returned to other European Union countries but no further unless their age is disputed and they are treated as adults. However, the UK and other EU states are now committed to returning some of these children at the point at which their applications for international protection is refused. This is a new departure as up until now states, including the UK, have offered domestic protection to children merely on the basis of their age. The decision to return unaccompanied children to their countries of origin gives rise to a number of issues about who should make such a decision, whether it will be compatible with domestic law and the UNCRC and what tests need to be developed to ensure that the best interests of these children are ascertained and acted upon.

References

AA (Afghanistan) v Secretary of State for the Home Department [2007] EWCA Civ 12.

Boland, K. (2010) *Children on the Move: A Report on Children of Afghan Origin Moving to Western Countries.* Available at www.unicef.org/infobycountry/files/Book_children_on_the_move.pdf

Boone, J. (2010) 'Afghan children dismiss diplomat's safer claim'. *The Guardian* 22 November 2010.

Crawley, H. (2007) *When is a Child Not a Child? Asylum, Age Disputes and the Process of Age Assessment.* London: ILPA.

Council of Europe (2005) *Convention on Action against Trafficking in Human Beings.* CETS No. 197. Warsaw: COE.

DCSF (2007) *Safeguarding Children from Abuse Linked to a Belief in Spirit Possession.* London: HMSO.

European Commission (2003) Council Regulation (EC) No. 343/2003 of 18 February establishing the criteria and mechanisms for determining the Member State responsible for examining and asylum application lodged in one of the Member States by a third-country national.

European Commission (2008) *Directive 2008/115/EC on the Common Standards and Procedures in Member States for Returning Illegally Staying Third Country Nationals,* 2008/115/EC.2008. Brussels: EC.

European Commission (2010) *Communication from the Commission to the European Parliament and the Council, Action Plan on Unaccompanied Minors (2010 – 2014)* SEC (2010) 534. Brussels: EC.

European Union (2000) *Charter of Fundamental Rights of the European Union,* 7 December 2000, Official Journal of the European Communities, 18 December 2000 (2000/C 364/01).

Home Office (2007) *Planning Better Outcomes and Support for Unaccompanied Asylum Seeking Children, Consultation Paper.* London: Home Office.

Home Office (2009) *Better Outcomes: The Way Forward. Improving the Care of Unaccompanied Asylum Seeking Children.* London: Home Office.

Home Office (2010) *UKBA:Processing an Asylum Application from a Child.* London: Home Office.

be ID and Others v Home Office [2005] EWCA Civ 38.

Kohli, R. (2006) 'The comfort of strangers: Social work practice with unaccompanied asylum seeking children and young people'. *Child and Family Social Work 11,* 1, 1–10.

Mougne, C. (2010) *Trees Only Move in the Wind: A Study of Unaccompanied Afghan Children in Europe.* Geneva: UNHCR.

R (on the application of TS) v The Secretary of State for the Home Department [2010] EWHC 2614 (Admin).

R (on the application of A) v National Asylum Support Service and another [2003] EWCA Civ 1473.

Rice, L. and Poppleton, S. (2009) *Policies on Reception, Return, Integration Arrangements for, and Numbers of, Unaccompanied Minors – UK Report for an EU Comparative Study.* London: Home Office, UKBA.

Travis, A. (2010) 'UK to deport child asylum seekers to Afghanistan'. *The Guardian* 7 June 2010.

UN High Commissioner for Refugees (2008) *UNHCR Guidelines on Determining the Best Interests of the Child.* Geneva: UNHCR.

UN High Commissioner for Refugees (2010a) *Baltic and Nordic Headlines: Deporting Asylum-seeking Children to Orphanages.* Accessed on 27 May 2011 at www.unhcr.se/Pdf/Baltic_nordic_HL_2010/March_2010.pdf

UN High Commissioner for Refugees (2010b) *Voices of Afghan Children: A Study on Asylum-Seeking Children in Sweden.* Geneva: UNHCR.

UNCRC (2005) *Treatment of Unaccompanied and Separated Children Outside Their Country of Origin* CRC/GC/2005/6 1 September 2005.

UNCRC (2008) *Concluding Observations United Kingdom of Great Britain and Northern Ireland.* Accessed on 21 July 2011 at http://media.education.gov.uk/assets/files/pdf/u/uncrc%20-%20third%20and%fourth%20concluding%20observations%202008.pdf

UNCROC (2005) General Comment No. 6 (2005): Treatment of Unaccompanied and Separated Children Outside Their Country of Origin. Accessed on 21 July 2011 available at http://tb.ohchr.org/default.aspx?Symbol=CRC/GC/2005/6

UNICEF (2005) *Statement on the UK Home Office 'Safe Returns to Albania' Pilot Project.* London.

UKBA (2008) *Afghanistan: Country of Origin Information Report.* London: UKBA.

ZH (Tanzania) (Appellant) v Secretary of State for the Home Department (Respondent) [2011] UKSC4, United Kingdom: Supreme Court 1 February 2011.

Chapter Eight

Listening to Separated Children

Emma Kelly

Introduction

This chapter considers the experiences of separated children through their own voices. To a degree, this group of children have been represented in research literature, although much of it is filtered through the eyes of another, usually an adult in a professional capacity (Chase 2010). While the views of professionals who work with separated children are significant and useful, they should be seen as distinct from what young people can tell us. A number of research studies have been undertaken to ascertain the views of separated children, although the subject is fraught with ethical and access issues. Not surprisingly, studies on the experiences of unaccompanied asylum seeking children (UASC) tend to predominate as they are a readily identifiable and definable group, unlike for instance accompanied minors. In general the research literature is tripartite, covering experiences pre-departure, the journey, and arrival and adapting to life in the UK.

While this review of the literature about separated children's experiences is not systematic in its intent, the aim has been to be thorough in the identification of research in this area. No exclusion criteria were applied other than that the research must involve the gathering of views, opinions and experiences directly from separated children up until 2010. This presents a challenge, given that different authors use different descriptions to capture this group of children including refugees, migrant children, children living with families who are seeking asylum and hidden children. Moreover, many of the studies cover the views of young people, who may now be in their twenties, and it is not always clear what proportion were under 18 on arrival in the UK. Most studies look at the accounts of adolescents (with a range from 11 to 18 years, with some stretching up to age 30) and overall there is a lacuna of information about younger children's experiences. Given the age range covered, the term 'young person' will be used throughout unless specifically addressing issues concerning younger children. In total nine empirical studies have been used in this chapter – seven written about separated children in the UK, one about young people in Ireland and one about separated children in Europe.

Ethical issues

Numerous ethical issues make this area difficult to research; however, some of these dilemmas are worth exploring as they have parallels with practitioners' experiences in gathering information about separated children. Hughman, Pittaway and Bartolomei (2011) argue that there are at least five reasons why practitioners should concern themselves with the quality and nature of research with refugees, three of which are relevant here. First, the need to avoid any trauma is central; this is one of the reasons given for the lack of qualitative research with child victims of trafficking (Pearce, Hynes and Bovarnick 2009). Also other researchers specifically choose not to ask separated children about their past because of the concern about reactivating trauma (Brownlees and Finch 2010). Second, young people may be rightly fearful of being identified through their comments, despite researchers' best efforts to anonymise their information; again, these concerns are particularly acute in the area of child trafficking. Third, potential interviewees also need to be clear about the purpose of the research and give their informed consent; however, this is a complicated process. Separated children may give their consent because they think that they will gain something from the process (such as successfully claiming asylum) or because they feel that they have to do what someone in authority asks them: 'the context of giving consent does have an impact on understanding, choice and so on. Autonomy is a capacity that is socially acquired and can be enhanced or undermined in many different ways' (Hughman *et al.* 2011, p.10). Finally, Adams (2009) challenges whether our intentions in hearing the child's voice can ever be truly honourable as in the process we make him or her the 'modern subject'; that is the object of our study.

Finding separated children

The studies show a bias towards collecting the views of UASC. This is not altogether surprising and reflects the relative accessibility of UASC. By definition, to seek asylum as a child entails both the Home Office (through the auspices of the United Kingdom Border Agency (UKBA)) and the local authority being aware of the child; data are collected for service provision, performance and budgetary management and border control. This does not actually mean that such data are always easy to find or that they are collected by central government, but at a local level those children who are defined as UASC are relatively easy to identify by researchers. Other children, such as those who have been trafficked, accompanied minors and children who have overstayed on a visa, present greater problems of identification (Brownlees and Finch 2010). By their very nature, these children are hidden from children's services. Even when there are suspicions that these children are, for instance, trafficked, it is difficult to transform the suspicion into a proven fact; for instance, very few children are defined at a national level as trafficked (Pearce *et al.* 2009).

To date there are no empirical research studies in the UK that consider the views of trafficked children, and all that has been written focuses on professionals' contact with these young people (Beddoe 2007; Brownlees and Finch 2010; Kelly 2009; Pearce *et al.* 2009). Few studies look at accompanied children, that is those children who either entered the UK with a relative or who have gone to live with an adult once in the UK. One study looks at the experiences of 'hidden children' in which '"hidden" is intended to refer to the unseen nature of the exploitation, the lack of awareness about these young people and the fact that exploiters deliberately act to keep them and their treatment hidden' (Wirtz 2009, p.5). Issues around access and ethics perhaps account for the small sample size of eight children who were formerly hidden and are now in receipt of local authority services, interviewed for Wirtz's (2009) study.

One of the surprises about the literature is the absence of information regarding EU migrant children. Individuals and families from European Economic Area (EEA) countries have a right to enter, live and work in the UK, although there are some exceptions for citizens from Bulgaria and Romania in relation to work (UKBA 2010). It is suspected that significant numbers of migrant children from the EEA and A8 (countries that joined the EU in 2003) enter the UK, either alone or accompanied by an unrelated adult; however, there are no recorded figures (Crawley 2006). In addition, the term 'migrant child' is often used broadly to describe a group of children similar to separated children (i.e. accompanied and trafficked minors) (Sigona and Hughes 2010). Data collected annually by the Child Exploitation and Online Protection Centre (CEOP) have tracked a rise in the number of children thought to be trafficked from EEA countries, with children identified from Romania, Poland, Bulgaria, Slovakia, Hungary and Portugal in 2010. Trafficked children from Eastern European countries tend to be female and are being sexually exploited commercially in the UK (CEOP 2010). There has been a particular focus on the trafficking of Roma children from Bulgaria and Romania with children identified primarily through law enforcement agencies, which perhaps explains the comments made by the UK government on the latest figures: 'The 32 children identified is almost certainly an underestimation of the scale and level of threat' (CEOP 2010, p.31).

Participation agenda

A child's right to be heard is enshrined in the United Nations Convention on the Rights of the Child (UNCRC), domestic law and policy. Despite these obligations, the second-class treatment of separated children is well documented, with all too frequently their immigration status taking precedence over their rights, views and needs as children (Burke 2010; Crawley 2006; Dennis 2002). The four Children's Commissioners have taken a particular interest in separated children and their lack of basic rights in the UK, documented in primary research into children's and professionals' views (Burke 2010; Children's Commissioner for England 2008; Kelly 2009; SCCYP and Perth UHI 2011) and a pilot scheme of guardianship for separated children in Scotland (see Chapter 9). The persistent agency and organisational barriers faced by separated children across diverse services such as health, children services and government agencies have been well documented. According to Burke (2010), separated children face barriers to participation at both strategic and individual levels, whether during immigration interviews, age assessments or while being held in detention centres.

Underpinning the debate about organisational barriers for separated children is the belief that children lack 'capacity', that is the ability to make complex decisions for themselves. Capacity is an interesting concept when applied to children, because a duality exists between the rights of all children to be heard and the rights of parents over children. Even in situations where parents are absent as with separated children, agency structures demand that someone (an adult) take 'best interest decisions' for a child. Despite the participation and child rights agenda, research based on talking to looked after children found that children are listened to with less attention than adults (Thomas and O'Kane 2000), which perhaps accounts for separated children's views that professionals have 'selective hearing' in relation to their needs and wishes (Wirtz 2009).

One of the key approaches to the literature is that children have the right not only to be heard but also to have their wishes acted on. While all who work with children in the UK will be familiar with the rhetoric of listening to children and ensuring their full participation, this can be extended to encompass the idea of 'child agency'. Conceptually, this moves beyond the universalist assumptions about rights to recognise that children have the ability to make significant decisions for themselves, including acting independently of their families. The 'conceptualisation of the child as an agent – capable of acting' (Whitehead, Hashim and Iversen 2007, p.4) is frequently used in the developing world, but it challenges western assumptions about the nature of childhood and the implied dependency and passivity of childhood.

According to Sigona and Hughes (2010), in our struggle to conceptualise separated children they are positioned either as vulnerable in need of protection or as bogus asylum seekers, who deliberately falsify claims. Similar binary constructions are recognised by Crawley (2010), who argues that separated children are seen both as passive victims with no agency and as a potential threat, so that the social constructions of childhood and asylum seeker collide creating unfavourable outcomes for separated children:

> current understanding of the experiences of separated asylum-seeking children is dominated by adult explanations and rationalisations which fail to engage directly with children and young people themselves. Separated asylum-seeking children are acted *upon* but they do not act: they are assumed to have no agency. (Crawley 2010, p.163)

The message from the literature is clear. Separated children may present as more resilient and advanced compared to equivalent looked after children in the UK (Chase, Knight and Statham 2008), yet they continue to receive services that have the effect of negating their sense of self by questioning the nature and veracity of their identify.

Credibility issues

Linked to the notion of listening to separated children is the often reported concern that they are not always credible. Indeed the literature suggests that many young people have experienced being disbelieved either by UKBA or children's services (Beddoe 2007; Brownlees and Finch 2010; Crawley 2006, 2007; Kelly 2009; Pearce *et al.* 2009). Inconsistency in narrative, inability to remember key events and elected silence are all taken at face value by some organisations, notably UKBA. Yet, evidence suggests that a number of complex factors are at play. First, trauma can lead to an individual being unable to (Zimmerman *et al.* 2006) or choosing to (Kohli 2006a) keep quiet about their experiences. Kohli (2006a) found on interviewing social workers about young people they were working with that all maintained silence over some aspects of their experiences: 'silence about the past was an organizing feature for many of them' (Kohli 2006a, p.713). Second, children may have been advised and warned not to tell authorities about their story and instead given false accounts to present when asked (Beddoe 2007; Crawley 2007); these can then conflict with a truer account given later on. Third, many young people may be uncertain as to why they are being asked such questions and of their potential significance. Fourth, some children may find it culturally unacceptable to talk about what has happened to them, especially if it has involved sexual abuse or exploitation (Pearce *et al.* 2009).

Departure experiences

Nearly all of the studies look at separated children's accounts of why they had to leave their country of origin. Although the accounts given are varied, the information is useful, because it fills a void that many practitioners face when working with separated children as accounts of their history are notoriously difficult to obtain. Some children chose not to talk about this aspect of their lives. Hopkins and Hill (2006) during their interviews with 31 young people (whose status was 15 discretionary leave, 6 indefinite leave to remain, 7 awaiting claim and 2 uncertain) in Scotland noted a general reticence on this subject and that 'the children displayed a range of degrees of openness with regards to discussing their previous experiences' (Hopkins and Hill 2006, p.30). They found that for the majority, someone else had made the decision that they should leave, although it is not clear who it was. Similar findings are reported by Chase *et al.* (2008) in their study of 54 young people, noting that children entered the UK as young as nine years of age.

In 2000, a major study for Save the Children looked at the experiences and accounts of separated children in Europe, with a specific focus on pre-departure accounts. Of the 218 young people, nearly half had originated from countries where there is armed conflict and a total of 441 possible movement reasons were given, with many children moving for multiple reasons. Reasons include separation of the child from parents (77), direct violence (70), children persecuted because of their political opinion or that of a family member (47), trafficked (26) and state sanctioned torture (25). This leads Ayotte (2000) to conclude that 'a striking feature of many cases was the complexity of reasons or contributory causes that resulted in children leaving their country' (Ayotte 2000, p.24).

A similarly distressing set of factors was found by Thomas, Nafees and Bhugra (2004) in their corroboration of young people's accounts in interviews, with legal and social work case notes. The sample in this study is large at 100, although it emerges that only two-thirds of the sample (67) was willing to be interviewed. Reasons given for not wanting to be interviewed were that the information was secret, that they did not want to talk about it or that they had experienced problems (Thomas *et al.* 2004). In exploring why children leave their country of origin, six main reasons are identified: death or persecution of family members, persecution of the young person, forced recruitment, war, trafficking and for a better education (the last group was made up of five children from African countries). The narratives of the young people highlight high levels of pre-departure violence (estimated at an average of 4.8 incidents per child), including torture, imprisonment and sexual violence. Of note is the level of sexual violence, given that over half the sample (59) were boys: 'of particular concern was the finding that a third (32%) of the young people included in this study reported being raped before leaving their country of origin, with around half of these reporting multiple rapes' (Thomas *et al.* 2004, p.119).

The stories told highlight the potential for traumatic events to have occurred pre-departure. However, Hopkins and Hill (2006) make the point that we should not assume a certain set of experiences for the child simply because a child comes from a certain country: often the child may come from a well-educated family but in a resource-poor country. Likewise, Chase (2010) points to the unique experiences that each separated child will have and that each child must be treated as such. While some of the young people in the study had experienced pre-departure traumatic events, others had not. In a narrative study of the stories of seven separated children, the theme of uniqueness is also prevalent:

> My young informants shared no common collective or personal histories of homeland or displacement from which cultural narratives of immigration are sometimes shaped. What the young people did share were a series of engagements with immigration, welfare and voluntary service institutions. (Adams 2009, p.166)

Experiences while en route

Similarly to pre-departure experiences, separated children tend to be reticent about their experiences during the journey to the UK. What is clear is that very few separated children know that they are travelling to the UK, with some asking their whereabouts on arrival. The assumption, supported by some evidence, is that most children do not travel alone even if they end up unaccompanied on arrival in the UK. According to Ayotte (2000), the majority of young people travelled with someone. Some children will be accompanied by a known adult, such as an extended family member, friend or humanitarian worker (Hopkins and Hill 2006), but others will be accompanied by someone who is an agent, or posing as related to the child (Ayotte 2000; Chase 2010). In part the difference depends on which country the child originated from, mode of transport used and what the intended purpose(s) of him or her coming to the UK are (Ayotte 2000; CEOP 2010). From the study of young people in Glasgow, Hopkins and Hill (2006) conclude:

> Almost all of the unaccompanied asylum-seeking children from Africa were brought by an agent, while the smaller number from Asia were either smuggled, or had to make their own way here without an agent. There may therefore be a more organised system of agents working in some of the African countries, with children from Asia having to adopt alternative strategies in order to seek safety. (Hopkins and Hill 2006, p.45)

The descriptions of children's journeys to the UK and Europe are varied. Some travel in relative safety, others experience hazardous conditions, including travelling as stowaways in boats and lorries, or being held temporarily in refugee camps. Chase *et al.* (2008) comment on 'the complexity and duration of their journeys', noting that some separated children travelled for several years before arriving in the UK (Chase *et al.* 2008, p.25). During transit, children may be subject to abuse, exploitation and neglect, which leads Ayotte to conclude that 'in many cases children face dangers in transit as serious as those they fled from' (Ayotte 2000, p.84).

Immigration status on arrival

Separated children arrive in the UK in a variety of ways, which in part reflect their immigration status. According to Ayotte (2000), the majority enter Europe with illegal documents or without documents; however, in the UK there are considerable data to show separated children passing through immigration control on either real or fake travel documents (CEOP 2010). For young people travelling from EEA areas, whether alone or accompanied, it is only the fact that they are bona fide members of the EEA that they need to demonstrate. Often difficulties arise just before or after the young people have passed through immigration control as their agent then abandons them (Beddoe 2007; Chase 2010). For some, the abandonment may be temporary and planned. Accounts of child victims of trafficking highlight that they are pre-warned of this plan and are expected to re-establish contact with the agent or someone else in the trafficking ring at a later stage (Beddoe 2007). Very few young people have spoken about this process, so it is based on a professional understanding in relation to patterns of young people going missing (Beddoe 2007; Pearce *et al.* 2009). For others, the abandonment is permanent as the agent has fulfilled their part of the contract by getting the children into the UK; numerous accounts have been documented of young people sleeping at airports or in city centres for several days before they either seek or attract assistance (Chase 2010; Stanley 2001). Other children enter the UK on a clandestine basis, usually hidden in the backs of lorries, from which some later escape or are released (CEOP 2010).

While some children will claim asylum at port of entry, the majority claim asylum later on (Home Office 2010), either once they have been abandoned or they have escaped abusive situations. For those young people who do come into contact with statutory services, including the police and immigration, their reception experiences are generally poor. Stanley (2001), in her study of the experiences of 125 young people seeking asylum in England, noted that at least one-quarter had 'chaotic experiences on arrival and received little or no support' (Stanley 2001, p.25). These experiences include being left to fend for themselves despite requesting support from the police, UKBA, children's services and surprisingly, according to Chase (2010), some NGOs. Other young people find themselves being detained by UKBA as adult asylum seekers or subject to dispersal according to the Immigration and Asylum Act 1999. In one case, the Children's Commissioner for England (2008) documented the experiences of a 15-year-old boy from Afghanistan whom he met at an asylum screening unit:

> He had been in the country for two days and had spent the night before last in a police station cell. He wanted to tell the police that he needed a shower, but was unable to do so because of the language barrier. He said that an Urdu interpreter had been provided, but that he could not understand him. He had no evidence to suggest which police station he had stayed at. (Children's Commissioner for England 2008, p.22)

Often separated children are befriended by strangers, who direct them to a voluntary agency or local authority service for support, leading Stanley to conclude that presenting at a specific children's services office is more 'as a result of chance rather than design' (Stanley 2001, p.25).

According to Hopkins and Hill (2006), young people spoke positively about the reception they received in Scotland but mentioned that they disliked the weather and poor accommodation (many had to wait some time to be in accommodation with cooking facilities). These two concerns, along with lack of familiar foods, run across many young people's narratives – 'at first I just got very cold, very cold, in fact I'm always cold here, even in the summer season it's never warm in England' (Adams 2009, p.163). Themes of acceptance emerged in the first study in Wales into the accounts of separated children in which 47 children and young people were interviewed, some of whom were part of a family group claiming asylum (Hewett *et al.* 2005). The young people reported not knowing much about Wales but experiencing a positive welcome on their arrival, with a nine-year-old male commenting: 'I thought it was going to be really fun just living in Wales because in London people don't talk to you but in Wales they talk to you more' (Hewett *et al.* 2005, p.33). According to Hewett *et al.* (2005), children who wanted to leave Wales gave their reasons as wanting to be in more diverse communities and having friends or family elsewhere in the UK.

Adaptation to life in the UK

Much has been written about how separated children adapt to life in the UK, although these studies tend to focus on the experiences of UASC, with the exception being a study by Brownlees and Finch (2010) for UNICEF UK; focusing on three local authority areas, the researchers interviewed 59 separated children between the ages of 13 and 23. However, this study acknowledges the difficulties in accessing potential interviewees as social workers acted as their gatekeepers (Brownlees and Finch 2010). Despite a professional preoccupation with assessment of the past, according to Kohli (2006b), most separated children are keen to focus on the present first, then the future, and finally the past. Research with nearly 200 young refugees (including separated children) supports this hypothesis. On being asked what they would most like from services, the researchers found overwhelmingly practical responses, including more help with language skills, help into school or college, spending more time with peers and more money (Princes Trust and Refugee Council 2003), while the need for practical information has been highlighted elsewhere (Brownlees and Finch 2010). Likewise in Hopkins and Hill's (2010) analysis of an earlier study, the young people's focus was very much on immediate needs.

Across much of the research similar issues covering the whole spectrum of separated children's needs are addressed, including accommodation, social care services, health services, immigration status and legal services, social isolation, resilience and moving on. These issues are explored as additional needs, relating to their status as separated children, on top of the needs common to all young people.

Accommodation

Dependent on age and to a certain extent local authority policy and resources, young people may be accommodated in foster care, residential care or private shared care (see Chapter 4). Clearly, accounts of such care will vary enormously from child to child and also reflect their preferred needs of caregiving. However, three key issues cut across all placement types. First, the child's perceptions of safety at the placement. Second, the degree to which the placement is or is not culturally appropriate. Third, distance of the placement from the local authority providing the service. Sense of safety is linked to both the nature of the placement and the previous experiences of the child (Hewett *et al.* 2005; Princes Trust and Refugee Council 2003). Residential (hostel and bed and breakfast type) care was felt to be more threatening than foster care, with separated children who were placed in hostels describing feelings of particular vulnerability: 'Hostel not too good really. Not at all. Food crap. English people there taking drugs...I was the youngest there [14] I had some friends my age. Four months at a hostel, two in a bedroom, shared bathroom...I didn't like it' (Stanley 2001, p.46).

One study identified a population of hidden homeless among separated children, defined as young people who were 'sofa surfing' or living in squats (Princes Trust and Refugee Council 2003). Echoes of similar concerns were noted in Wales, when separated children were refused asylum and 'disappeared' into the informal economy (Hewett *et al.* 2005). Children who had been trafficked can be left with residual feelings of paranoia and distrust; many found it hard to believe that their foster carer or residential carer worker had their best interests at heart (Fursland 2009). Some separated children report positive experiences of 'matching', but Chase (2010) concludes that matching needs are less important than the quality of the relationship that develops between the child and the foster carer. In addition, pressures on local services and lack of placement availability, combined with concerns about community resources and integration, have led some local authorities to seek placements for separated children outside of their area (Hewett *et al.* 2005).

Healthcare provision

The type of healthcare provision available to separated children partly depends on their status; looked after children will benefit from a full medical, whereas children who are intentionally hidden may go for years without their basic health needs being met. Surprisingly one of the main preoccupations across many of the studies is a concern about diet and food, although issues such as access to a GP and secondary health services are also raised (Brownlees and Finch 2010). The concern is less about the availability of traditionally significant foods, although some children did lament not being able to eat specific foods, but more about lack of facilities and money. Many separated children comment on poor or non-existent cooking facilities in their accommodation, resulting in them relying on takeaway food (Brownlees and Finch 2010; Hopkins and Hill 2006). Hewett *et al.* (2005) give an example of a young person who had lived in a hostel for 13 months and throughout that time had to rely on fast food. A lack of knowledge about how to cook also led some young people to rely on takeaway food, which is invariably unhealthy and costly.

Social care provision

In general, accounts of children's services are very mixed, with some separated children making it clear that they valued the time and effort that their social worker put in. However, evidence of mistrust and confusion is also clear in accounts of contact with children's services. Principally, this mistrust emerges through choosing not to share information with their social worker, either because they did not trust them or because they were never asked during monitoring visits, as described by this young female hidden in a private fostering situation: 'Useless. So many opportunities and they missed it. I would have been like Baby P' (Wirtz 2009, p.35). Lack of trust stemmed from previous experiences of statutory services in their country of origin, uncertainty about the role and function of children's services in the UK and the association that was made between social services and immigration. This distrust may increase with age, with Chase (2010) noting that those close to age 18 were also 'more mistrustful of the interplay between social care and immigration services' (Chase 2010, p.2060). Irrespective of the reality of the relationship between social services and UKBA, for separated children they were linked, both forming a part of the 'surveillance systems' that they describe being continually a part of (Chase 2010).

Educational provision

The provision of education to separated children is essential, although young people report varied experiences in relation to access. What is clear from all the literature is the value that separated children place on education, with some young people commenting that they would rather do extra study than any other extracurricular activity (Dunkerley *et al.* 2006). Other authors suggest that 'education is the key to their successful adulthood and, we might speculate it is something with which to gain control and stability through the normalising activity of school in an otherwise unpredictable situation' (Maegusuku-Hewett *et al.* 2007, p.315). Provision should be automatic for under 16s but for young people aged 16 plus, there are far fewer opportunities. Young people report having to attend adult language classes with little else available for them. Restricted access to mainstream education impacts on social integration, both in a day-to-day sense and in that young people do not have the opportunity to develop their language skills. As one unaccompanied minor said, 'I want to work and go to college, go to university one day. Yes, I have dreams' (Hopkins and Hill 2010, p.402).

Talking about it all …

Evidence emerges across the literature that separated children are very selective about whom they talk to about their experiences and about the experiences they choose to reveal. Separated children's silence is particularly acute, with 'state' services such as UKBA, but even with friends, separated children seem to be reticent to talk about their experiences. According to Chase (2010), some young people told friends some aspects of their past, but never all. Underpinning this reticence, it is argued that young people need to create a story that fits, or indeed one that makes them fit more easily into their social environment. Adams (2009) argues that this storytelling is essential in the management of their 'life-chances'. In a similar vein, Kohli (2006a) describes it as the 'thin stories' that children actively present; 'while the thick stories might be multi-layered and complex, it is the simpler thin stories that are perceived as being admissible to the receiving authorities', which are stories about the need for protection from suffering (Kohli 2006a, p.711). Some young people indicate that they do not want to talk about the past because it is too difficult, such as Hellen from Ethiopia:

> Sometimes they don't understand you when you are sad. They keep asking you questions. It makes me angry; it makes me want

> to shout. It makes me remember all the bad things and they don't understand that. If they ask me [questions] I will suffer for months. (Chase 2010, p.2060)

For other separated children, hiding the past is a way of reducing the perceived stigma of being an asylum seeker, so they develop strategies to resist that label, usually by not telling anyone of their status even when they have been in the UK for some period of time. Adams suggests 'a common story of radical and irreconcilable social dislocation' (Adams 2009, p.161) in the seven children she interviewed; these children actively presented a sharp distinction between the past and their present life in the UK, even when there might be mediating aspects such as access to TV channels native to their country.

Not surprisingly many separated children give accounts of being socially isolated and lonely (Chase *et al.* 2008; Hewett *et al.* 2005; Hopkins and Hill 2006), with one young person commenting: 'Well, I suppose I'm not having any friends. The woman and the shopkeeper are my friends at the moment' (Hewett *et al.* 2005, p.34). According to Hopkins and Hill (2006), these feelings are exacerbated by differences in language and culture, experience of racism and uncertainty of asylum application. One study, which compares the views of unaccompanied minors with those in families, challenges this view, noting that 'young people arriving in the UK alone or with strangers appeared to be more ambivalent towards public opinion. Almost twice as many young people who travelled unaccompanied stated that they are unaffected by what the public think of them', which the authors suggest may be a result of 'intensity of their experiences and sense of self-preservation' (Princes Trust and Refugee Council 2003, p.11).

Adaptation and resilience

> But I'm trying to keep my head up... You know, because I know things one day are gonna get better. You know I mean, so... I'm hopeful. It won't be this way every day. It won't. (Raillaigh and Gilligan 2010, p.230)

In listening to separated children's voices, considerable aspects of strength and resilience have been identified, including the desire to learn, the ability to work hard as well as an optimistic outlook. The literature on resilience in separated children is complicated given that it has the potential to suggest a set of typical winning characteristics but as Maegusuku-Hewett *et al.* (2007) point out, resilience strategies in one child may manifest themselves at different times and ways in another child. Drawing on the data for a Save the Children study in Wales, Maegusuku-Hewett *et al.* (2007) explore two aspects of coping strategies that were revealed in the narratives of the young people; namely personal attributes and a positive cultural identity. Some of the young people demonstrated optimism and a belief that they were capable of actively overcoming prejudice, hardship and adversity, both at a personal level and in relation to external factors such as cultural difference. This leads Maegusuku-Hewett *et al.* (2007) to conclude: 'it is the collective sense of having a particular cultural identity that supports resilience in many stressful environments'(Maegusuku-Hewett *et al.* 2007, p.315).

In a similar vein, Raillaigh and Gilligan (2010) propose that separated children actively choose their coping strategies:

> The narratives of the participants suggested that the coping strategies that they used were purposefully chosen as they believed them to be the most compelling options available in their circumstances. As such, the participants were active in their efforts to survive. (Raillaigh and Gilligan 2010, p.233)

Collecting data through interviews from 31 young people living in lodges in Ireland, six active coping strategies are identified. These six strategies include the need to maintain continuity in a changed context, adjustment by learning, adopting a positive outlook, suppressing emotions and seeking distractions, acting independently and distrusting agencies. What surprised the authors was the central importance of religion as an underpinning coping strategy, with 30 of 31 young people mentioning the role of their faith. These findings are significant, giving practitioners' insight into the importance of religious beliefs and the need to ensure that these are assessed accurately and never undermined.

Conclusion

The voices of separated children are there to be heard. It remains an irony that so much social work and other childcare practice is dominated by expressions of the difficulty in 'making' young people talk, when the views, attitudes, experiences and hopes of separated children have been so clearly captured both in the UK and elsewhere in Europe. The remarkable consistency of accounts given about time in the UK is striking. Throughout the studies, separated children have told us about their poor experiences at the hands of statutory services, of our professional obsession in wanting a full disclosure while being provided with substandard accommodation and support. Our responses to such accounts are underpinned by uncertainty about how to conceptualise separated children and indeed all children. Are they victims in need of protection or young people capable of making significant decisions? Practice responses indicate that we are uncomfortable with uncertainty and ambiguity, wanting a child to be one or the other, and never both. Yet current English and Welsh guidance is clear that we can recognise both these roles for separated children by safeguarding children *and* promoting their welfare.

References

Adams, M. (2009) 'Stories of fracture and claim for belonging: Young migrants' narratives of arrival in Britain'. *Children's Geographies 7*, 2, 159–171.

Ayotte, W. (2000) *Separated Children Coming to Western Europe: Why They Travel and How They Arrive.* London: Save the Children.

Beddoe, C. (2007) *Missing Out: A Study of Child Trafficking in the North-West, North- East and West Midlands.* London: ECPAT.

Brownlees, L. and Finch, N. (2010) *Levelling the Playing Field: A UNICEF UK Report into Provision of Services to Unaccompanied or Separated Migrant Children in Three Local Authority Areas in England.* London: UNICEF UK.

Burke, T. (2010) *Anyone Listening? Evidence of Children and Young People's Participation in England.* London, CRAE.

Chase, E. (2010) 'Agency and silence: Young people seeking asylum alone in the UK'. *British Journal of Social Work 40*, 7, 2050–2068.

Chase, E., Knight, A. and Statham, J. (2008) *The Emotional Wellbeing of Unaccompanied Young People Seeking Asylum in the UK.* London: BAAF.

Child Exploitation and Online Protection Centre (CEOP) (2010) *Strategic Threat Assessment: Child Trafficking in the UK.* London: CEOP.

Children's Commissioner for England (2008) *Claiming Asylum at a Screening Unit as an Unaccompanied Child.* London: 11 Million.

Crawley, H. (2006) *Child First, Migrant Second: Ensuring that Every Child Matters.* London: Immigration Law Practitioners' Association.

Crawley, H. (2007) *When is a Child Not a Child? Asylum, Age Disputes and the Process of Age Assessments.* London: Immigration Law Practitioners' Association.

Crawley, H. (2010) '"No one gives you a chance to say what you are thinking": Finding space for children's agency in the UK asylum system'. *Area 42*, 2, 162–169.

Dennis, J. (2002) *A Case for Change: How Refugee Children in England are Missing Out.* London: The Refugee Council.

Dunkerley, D., Scourfield, J., Maegaesku-Hewett, T. and Smalley, N. (2006) 'Children seeking asylum in Wales'. *Journal of Refugee Studies 19*, 4, 488–508.

Fursland, E. (2009) *Caring for a Young Person who has been Trafficked: A Guide for Foster Carers.* London: BAAF.

Hewett, T., Smalley, N., Dunkerley, D. and Scourfield J. (2005) *Uncertain Futures: Children Seeking Asylum in Wales.* Cardiff: Save the Children.

Home Office (2010) *Control of Immigration: Statistics United Kingdom, 2009.* Accessed on 31 May 2011 at www.homeoffice.gov.uk/publications/science-research-statistics/research-statistics/immigration-asylum-research/hosb1510/hosb1510?view=Binary

Hopkins, P. and Hill, M. (2006) *'This Is a Good Place to Live and Think about the Future': The Needs and Experiences of Unaccompanied Asylum-Seeking Children and Young People in Scotland.* Glasgow: Scottish Refugee Council.

Hopkins, P. and Hill, M. (2010) 'The needs and strengths of unaccompanied asylum-seeking children and young people in Scotland'. *Child and Family Social Work 15*, 4, 399–408.

Hughman, R., Pittaway, E. and Bartolomei, L. (2011) 'When "Do no harm" is not enough: The ethics of research with refugees and other vulnerable groups'. *British Journal of Social Work Advance Access (2011)* 1–17. Available at http://bjsw.oxfordjournals.org/content/early/2011/03/01/bjsw.bcr013.full.pdf+html, accessed 13 October 2010.

Kelly, E. (2009) *Bordering on Concern: Child Trafficking in Wales.* Swansea: Children's Commissioner for Wales and ECPAT UK.

Kohli, R. (2006a) 'The sound of silence: Listening to what unaccompanied asylum seeking children say and do not say'. *British Journal of Social Work 36*, 5, 707–721.

Kohli, R. (2006b) 'The comfort of strangers: Social work practice with unaccompanied asylum-seeking children and young people in the UK'. *Child and Family Social Work 11*, 1, 1–10.

Maegusuku-Hewett, T., Dunkerley, D., Scourfield, J. and Smalley, N. (2007) Refugee children in Wales: Coping and adaption in the face of adversity. *Children and Society 21*, 309–321.

Pearce, J., Hynes, P. and Bovarnick, S. (2009) *Breaking the Wall of Silence: Practitioners' Responses to Trafficked Children.* University of Bedfordshire and NSPCC.

Princes Trust and Refugee Council (2003) *Starting Over: Young Refugees Talk about Life in Britain.* London: Princes Trust.

Raillaigh, M. and Gilliagan, R. (2010) 'Active survival in the lives of unaccompanied minors: Coping strategies, resilience, and the relevance of religion'. *Child and Family Social Work 15*, 2, 226–237.

Scotland's Commissioner for Children and Young People (SCCYP) and Perth UHI (2011) *A Scoping Study into the Nature and Extent of Child Trafficking in Scotland.* Edinburgh: SCCYP.

Sigona, N. and Hughes, V. (2010) *Being Children and Undocumented in the UK: A Background Paper.* Oxford: COMPAS, University of Oxford.

Stanley, K. (2001) *Cold Comfort: Young Separated Refugees in England.* London: Save the Children.

Thomas, N. and O'Kane, C. (2000) 'Discovering what children think: Connections between research and practice'. *British Journal of Social Work 30*, 6, 819–835.

Thomas, S.B., Nafees, B. and Bhugra, D. (2004) '"I was running away from death": The pre-flight experiences of unaccompanied asylum-seeking children in the UK'. *Child Care Health and Development 30*, 2, 113–122.

United Kingdom Border Agency (UKBA) (2010) *Information for Bulgarian and Romanian Nationals.* Accessed on 18 July 2011 at www.ukba.homeoffice.gov.uk/workingintheuk/eea/bulgariaromania/liveworkuk/

Whitehead, A., Hashim, I. and Iversen, I. (2007) *Child Migration, Child Agency and Inter-generational Relations in Africa and South Asia.* University of Sussex: Development Research Centre on Migration, Globalisation and Poverty.

Wirtz, L. (2009) *Hidden Children – Separated Children at Risk.* London: The Children's Society.

Zimmerman, C., Hossain, M., Yun, K., Roche, B., Morrison, L. and Watts, C. (2006) *Stolen Smiles: The Physical and Psychological Health Consequences of Women and Adolescents Trafficked into Europe.* London: London School of Hygiene and Tropical Medicine.

Chapter Nine

The Role of the Guardian for Separated Children

Stefan Stoyanov

Introduction

The particular vulnerabilities of separated children result in equal measure from the circumstances of their separation from their families in their countries of origin, experiences during the journeys they undertake before they reach their destination (often unknown to them) and challenges they face in the countries of destination related to their welfare, education and legal needs. The situation of separated children is described as 'a matter of urgent concern' in a Recommendation of the Parliamentary Assembly of the Council of Europe (Council of Europe 2005, para. 3).

The recognition of these vulnerabilities and the states' obligations stemming from the universally recognised human rights of separated children have led to recommendations for providing this group of children with guardians in destination countries to improve their protection and help them navigate the complex immigration and care systems they encounter. Such calls have been made by national and international institutions, non-governmental and intergovernmental organisations and networks, and are reflected in international and domestic law and guidance.

This chapter provides an overview of the recommendations and existing systems of guardianship for separated children, reviews their basic rights and looks at the various notions of guardianship. It also explores what form guardianship has taken in different European countries and analyses the debate in the UK and the Separated Children Guardianship in Scotland pilot project.

Rights premises

The United Nations Convention on the Rights of the Child (UNCRC) requires that the governments which have signed up to it ensure that children are protected against all forms of discrimination on the basis of their status (Article 2), including their immigration status. Article 20 entitles children deprived of their families to special protection and assistance. More specifically, Article 22 commits state parties to provide appropriate protection and humanitarian assistance for asylum seeking and refugee children (UNCRC 1989).

The UN Committee on the Rights of the Child (CRC) issued a General Comment on the treatment of separated children outside their country of origin in 2005 which calls for the appointment of guardians or advisers to represent an unaccompanied child's best interests (CRC 2005). The General Comment provides a concrete vision of a guardian's remit and expertise where he or she 'serves as a key procedural safeguard to ensure respect for the best interests of an unaccompanied or separated child' (CRC 2005, p.9). CRC (2005) recommends that a guardian should be appointed from as early as a separated child is identified and should have responsibility for the child until she or he turns 18 or is removed from the UK. The role of the guardian is of such importance that the referral of a child for asylum or any other procedures before the appointment of a guardian is discouraged (CRC 2005).

The requirement for the appointment of guardians for separated children is present in a number of other international documents to which the UK is party. Article 10 (4a) of the Council of Europe (2005) Convention on Action against Trafficking in Human Beings, for example, calls for the appointment of 'a legal guardian, organisation or authority, which shall act in the best interests of that child as soon as a separated child is identified as a victim'. Of note here is the need for prompt action and for representing the child's best interests. Similar requirements are to be found in EU directives, to which the UK is a party.

International guidelines

All UN bodies and international organisations promoting the rights of separated children have highlighted the need for guardians to improve their protection and support their asylum claim. In 1997 the UN High Commissioner for Refugees (UNHCR) produced *Guidelines on Policies and Procedures in Dealing with Unaccompanied Children Seeking Asylum*. The guidelines call for the establishment of independent organisations with formal accreditation that would be responsible for the appointment of guardians for separated children from the moment of their identification. The role envisaged for the guardian is one of a link between the child and the various agencies involved in meeting his or her 'legal, social, medical and psychological needs' (UNHCR 1997, p.7).

More recent *UNHCR Guidelines on Determining the Best Interests of the Child* (UNHCR 2008) recognise the need to include guardians in representing the child in judicial proceedings and in the process of best interest determination by attending panel sessions (UNHCR 2008, p.55).

The joint *Statement of Good Practice* by UNHCR, the Separated Children in Europe Programme (SCEP) and Save the Children Alliance presents a comprehensive picture of the possible scope of responsibilities of guardians. These include ensuring that all decisions have the child's best interests as a primary consideration, that the child's views and opinions are considered in all decisions that affect him or her, that the child is receiving suitable care, education and legal representation as well as contributing to a durable solution in the child's best interests (SCEP 2008). UNICEF (2006) has also called for the allocation of guardians to child victims of trafficking in its *Guidelines on the Protection of Child Victims of Trafficking*.

Demands for guardianship in the UK

CRC has recommended the appointment of guardians for children in two consecutive concluding observations in response to the UK's second (2002) and its consolidated third and fourth reports (2008).

The UK government's response to the 2002 recommendation was that there is no need to appoint guardians as adequate arrangements for the care and protection of separated children already exist (UK Government 2007). It concludes that 'given the support provided to children and young people under the provisions it outlines in its response, the Government does not believe that a formal "guardianship scheme" is necessary' (UK Government 2007, p.131). A written answer to a parliamentary question by a member of the House of Lords in 2007 makes it clear that the same view applies in relation to guardianship for child victims of trafficking (Hansard HC vol 5 516 cols WA3, 16 July 2007).

This view is not shared by many UK children's rights and refugee organisations and institutions, including those which provide direct care and support to separated children (CRAE 2008). The UK Children's Commissioners' (2008) Report to CRC summarises well most of the arguments of those disagreeing with the government's position:

> We disagree with the UK Government's assertion that a
> formal 'guardianship scheme' is not necessary or that existing
> arrangements are adequate. Many asylum seeking children are not
> allocated their own social worker and while the Children's Panel
> of Advisers provides an excellent service in England, it has no
> statutory role and is unable to meet the demand for its services. A
> legal guardian should be appointed as soon as an unaccompanied
> asylum seeking child is identified and the arrangement maintained
> until the child reaches 18 or has permanently left the UK. Despite
> asylum policy being reserved to the UK Government, the Scottish
> Government has begun to develop a new model for dealing with
> unaccompanied minors, which is to be welcomed. (UK Children's
> Commissioners 2008, p.30)

The four Children's Commissioners go on to recommend that 'the UK
Government should ensure that children whose claims fail are only ever
removed if it is in their best interests as ascertained by a UK appointed legal
guardian' (UK Children's Commissioners 2008, p.32)

Similar views are shared by the members of the Refugee Children's
Consortium (RCC 2007), a wide coalition of children's and refugee
organisations. The Immigration Law Practitioners' Association describes the
lack of guardianship as a 'desperate lacuna, affecting support entitlements
as well as the child's ability to pursue the claim to asylum' (ILPA 2006,
p.7). Such a claim is substantiated in detail by the evidence provided in
the Sixth Report to the Minister by the UNHCR (2009) *Quality Initiative
Project*. The UNHCR Representation in the UK has been supporting the
UK government's efforts to improve the quality of United Kingdom Border
Agency's (UKBA) asylum decision making through its *Quality Initiative
Project* since 2004.

The report cites a number of cases in which the best interests of separated
asylum seeking children have been apparently left without consideration to
the detriment of the child's asylum case. It found 'lack of formal procedure
for assessing whether obtaining evidence from an asylum-seeking child
above the age of 12 through interview may or may not be in the child's
best interests' (UNHCR 2009, p.34). This resulted in interviewing children
who were not able to provide evidence in support of their asylum claim
at an interview or were unfit to be interviewed for other reasons, while at
the same time other children who would have been able to support their
asylum claim at an interview were denied this opportunity:

> In one claim, for example, a 14-year-old explained in her
> statement that, after having been the victim of rape, a state of

shock had led to her not speaking for four months. UNHCR was disappointed to note that there was no indication from the information available to UNHCR that consideration had been given to the fact that she had suffered trauma and that this may have impacted upon her ability to provide evidence via interview. (UNHCR 2009, p.35)

The above example demonstrates a gap in best interest determination that would best be filled by a guardian role. Child victims of trafficking, separated or not, are a particularly vulnerable group in an area where both policy and practice leave a lot to be desired (Anti-Trafficking Monitoring Group 2010). For that reason organisations campaigning for the rights of trafficked children are demanding the appointment of guardians to this vulnerable group, in line with the stipulations of the Council of Europe Convention on Action against Trafficking in Human Beings (Anti-Trafficking Monitoring Group 2010; Sillen and Beddoe 2007).

Notwithstanding all the above demands for the appointment of guardians with separated children, the UK government's position for the time being remains unchanged (House of Commons 2011). Two developments in the UK since 2008, however, are worth noting as they remove some of the obstacles to protection of separated children arriving in the UK and could, in the long run, facilitate the introduction of guardianship for separated children in the UK.

In 2008, the UK withdrew its general reservation to the UNCRC regarding children subject to immigration control. The reservation had allowed the UK government to selectively apply the UNCRC with regards to separated children. Section 11 of the Children Act 2004 places a duty on a wide range of bodies, whose work affects children in England, to safeguard and promote the welfare of children when discharging their functions. After years of campaigning by non-governmental organisations (NGOs) calling for this duty to apply to staff and contractors of the UKBA, a new duty was introduced in Section 55 of the Borders, Citizenship and Immigration Act 2009. It stipulates that UKBA and its contractors should perform their functions with regard to the need to safeguard and promote the welfare of children who are in the UK.

Guardianship in the UK

Views of stakeholders remain split on the question whether a new (guardianship) institution is needed to ensure adequate care provision for separated children or a way can be found to remedy the situation by using the existing roles and mechanisms (Save the Children UK 2008). One of the complications is that the use of the term 'guardian' causes some confusion because it already has different meanings in the various jurisdictions of the UK. Independent adviser is another possible name for this type of service. Some, including in the UK coalition government, believe that independent reviewing officers (IROs) fulfil the role of ensuring looked after children receive adequate care (Hansard HC Deb c48WH, 12 October 2010). It is often forgotten that the role of IRO exists only in England and Wales. There are issues related to the workload and therefore the accessibility of IROs for looked after children, which diminishes their ability to challenge inadequate local authority arrangements for the care of separated children (Save the Children UK 2008). However, concerns regarding their independence from local authorities are thought to have been addressed with amendments to arrangements regarding IROs made under the Children and Young Persons Act 2008.

The perceptions of what form guardianship in the UK should take can be roughly divided into three groups. First, the view that appears to be shared by a majority of stakeholders is of guardianship as a statutory role in which the guardian has the power to represent the child's best interests and to be involved in any decision making affecting the child's future. Second, the view is of the guardian as a befriender supporting the child. Third, some see advocacy as the core function of a guardian. NGOs see the independence from both central government and local authorities as another key feature of guardianship (Save the Children UK 2008).

Separated children themselves have been seldom asked for their views on guardianship. One exception is the consultation held by ECPAT UK with its peer support group for child victims of trafficking, whose members were asked what they needed to feel safe and what their views were on guardianship. The responses indicated the young people's need for a designated person whom they can talk to, confide in and who does not change frequently (ECPAT UK 2010).

The series of consultations with separated children run by the Scottish Refugee Council in preparation for its Separated Children Guardianship in Scotland Pilot is the other exception. During the initial consultations young people were asked what form guardianship should take to make a difference in their lives. The issues the young people in this consultation needed help with included the speed of the asylum process; the process-led (as opposed to child-centred) nature of the asylum system, their lack of awareness of their rights and of concepts of welfare and social work; the asylum system's apparent culture of disbelief and young people's problems in understanding the meaning of the letters informing them of decisions on their asylum status and other paperwork. Young people also stated they needed help with understanding their appeal rights (Scottish Refugee Council and Aberlour Childcare Trust 2009). These views have informed the development of the first project piloting a guardianship service in the UK, described below.

Scottish guardianship pilot

The first pilot of a guardianship service started in the summer of 2010 in Scotland. The two-and-a-half-year project, co-funded by the Scottish government, is run by Scottish Refugee Council in partnership with Aberlour Childcare Trust, with the latter delivering the service and being responsible for the project's operational management.

The two main outcomes sought are, first, to significantly improve the experience of the immigration and child welfare processes for the children covered by the pilot, and second, to develop a child-centred model of practice that 'promotes improved interagency working within the immigration and child welfare processes, meeting relevant UNHCR guidelines; improves the quality of information upon which the UKBA decision-making process is based; provides benefits that would be applicable beyond Scotland' (Scottish Refugee Council and Aberlour Childcare Trust 2009, p.18).

The project aims to offer guardianship services to all newly arriving separated children located within two hours' travel from Glasgow, which would in practice mean 98 per cent coverage of all separated children arriving in Scotland. It will also engage with the current cohort of separated children in Glasgow by 'providing group briefings at critical stages of the asylum process' (Scottish Refugee Council and Aberlour Childcare Trust 2009, p.25). In the second year of implementation the project will offer a telephone information support and guidance service to local authorities, health boards and other relevant bodies. It will also produce a practice manual to assist other agencies in rolling out similar services (Scottish Refugee Council and Aberlour Childcare Trust 2009).

The guardian will 'consistently support the child through the asylum process from the first step' (Scottish Refugee Council and Aberlour Childcare Trust 2009, p.26), which will include support for those whose age is disputed. They will be 'a consistent point of professional contact ensuring that the child's best interests are taken into account in all decision-making affecting them' (Scottish Refugee Council and Aberlour Childcare Trust 2009, p.4). The project description provides a detailed overview of the types of interventions that guardians will be involved in during the different stages of the separated children's stay in Scotland. Another aspect that would determine the effectiveness of guardians in ensuring a child's best interests being considered would be the project's success in agreeing to involve guardians in discussions with the UKBA regarding any plans to return the child to his or her country of origin. This would depend on the policy instructions developed centrally by UKBA and on the flexibility of the regional office of the agency.

The project has established an action research methodology with ongoing monitoring and evaluation provided by two noted academics. An early round of evaluation activities has already taken place and the evaluators are satisfied with the project's progress in terms of establishing a project management framework, and the appointment of motivated and suitably qualified guardians (Kohli and Crawley 2010). The evaluators note good levels of cooperation with the UKBA during the early stages of the project. They note the fluidity in the working definition of guardianship and the guardians' role and discuss the perceived and actual difficulties in guardians being accepted by other professionals involved with the same children. These professionals may be more difficult to engage with if they see the guardian's role as duplicating or endangering their own role (Kohli and Crawley 2010). The project has time to produce a definition of guardianship based on its successes and the lessons it will learn in the course of its implementation.

Guardianship in other European countries

Notwithstanding Council of Europe conventions and resolutions or EU directives calling for the establishment of guardianship systems, guardianship is far from being common, not only in wider Europe but also among the old members of the European Union (Alikhan and Floor 2007; Vestegen and Murk 2010). The existence of a guardianship system in a country is not in itself an indicator that separated children are better cared for or more fairly treated in asylum decision making. The types and the quality of care arrangements differ significantly from country to country and those variations are not linked to the existence of guardians. The types of duties and powers of guardians and their actual involvement also vary significantly between (and sometimes within) the different countries (Alikhan and Floor 2007; Vestegen and Murk 2010). This chapter is not showcasing a particular model of guardianship as a good example for the UK because even in the case of models of guardianship seen to be working well in some European countries, such 'success' is closely linked to the particular childcare and asylum legal policy models in those countries and child-related legal architecture; taken out of that particular context they may not work so well elsewhere. Instead, we look at different models of guardianship and the specifics that characterise these models in different countries.

While some countries provide care similar to that provided to citizen children deprived of parental care, other countries have developed special facilities for the accommodation of separated children seeking asylum (Alikhan and Floor 2007). To make any conclusions about differential treatment, however, is difficult, as this would require comparisons with the different forms of childcare and child protection provided to national children, the national trends for placements in, for example, foster care as opposed to placements in residential care or semi-independent facilities and the ages at which these types of placements are likely to occur. In some cases, however, it is clear that separated children are being treated as migrants first and children second as exemplified by the practice of holding children in waiting zones at airports for over a week in France (Vestegen and Murk 2010).

Independence of guardians

For a guardian to be able to influence decisions in consideration of the best interests of the child, and to advocate for the most suitable form of care and education to be provided to the separated child, his or her independence from immigration and local authorities is crucial. It is equally important that the guardian has no vested interest, that is financial interest, in any decisions affecting the child. Some of the more independent systems of guardianship in the EU are thought to be in Sweden, Germany and the Netherlands (Alikhan and Floor 2007; Vestegen and Murk 2010).

Voluntary or professional

Most countries in Europe have a preference for professional forms of guardianship (Alikhan and Floor 2007). The Netherlands uses professional guardians. Sweden uses voluntary ones, while in countries like Belgium and Germany, both models coexist (Alikhan and Floor 2007). Professional guardians are employed either by a state institution with responsibility for separated children or for immigration in general, or by NGOs (Alikhan and Floor 2007).

In 9 (21.4%) of the 42 countries studied by UNHCR there were no clearly defined, or any at all, criteria regarding guardians' qualifications. In 10 (24%) of the countries they were expected to have a social work background and in 6 (14%) a legal background.

Duties of guardians

The main division in the types of duties of guardians is between those who primarily provide legal representation and those who are expected to ensure the welfare of the child. This division is not, however, clear-cut. Overall, the most common duties are found to be related to 'care arrangements, accommodation and health' (Alikhan and Floor 2007, p.13). The duties would also depend on whether the guardianship assignment is temporary or until a durable solution has been found. In some countries (e.g. Belgium), the guardian has responsibility for the age assessment of the separated child. In other countries, like Germany, a guardian is allocated only after the age assessment has confirmed that the asylum applicant is a child (Vestegen and Murk 2010).

Since most international documents refer to the guardian's role as being about involvement in the determination of the child's best interests, it is somewhat disappointing that not all guardians fulfil this role; in only 24 (57%) of the 42 countries studied by UNHCR, guardians, or their equivalents, had such a duty (Vestegen and Murk 2010). This is also the case with guardians' involvement in identification of durable (long-term) solutions: 18 of the countries studied had such a duty for guardians (Vestegen and Murk 2010).

Conclusion

The different types of guardianship and, consequently, the different duties of guardians across Europe do not allow for a single definition of guardianship to be adopted (Vestegen and Murk 2010).

Systems of guardianship or systems providing a service equivalent to guardianship vary significantly in different country contexts. Often the formally adopted models also differ from what is happening in practice (Vestegen and Murk 2010). Therefore, any endorsement of a model as suitable for the UK context risks proving counterproductive. Similarly, any attempt at harmonising guardianship policies and practices in the EU could result in a race to the bottom where the adopted features of a common model are worse than the arrangements currently available in many countries.

The Scottish pilot is encouraging both in terms of the practical domestic knowledge it will bring about and in terms of the political will to respond positively to the recommendations of the UNCRC demonstrated by the Scottish government. The good cooperation with UKBA is also commendable, although the real test for the relationship with UKBA will be the extent to which it will agree to consult guardians when it comes to determining the best interests of the children in the project.

The 2008 withdrawal of the UK general reservation to the UNCRC regarding children subject to immigration control, together with the introduction of a new duty for the UKBA in Section 55 of the Borders, Citizenship and Immigration Act 2009 to safeguard and promote the welfare of children who are in the UK, gives reason for hope that the UK is firmly, if slowly, moving towards providing better protection for separated children. The next logical step in that direction would be to identify the best possible ways of complying with the UNCRC recommendations and the numerous calls by organisations and institutions supporting the rights of separated children by introducing a system of legal guardianship in the UK.

References

Alikhan, S. and Floor, M. (2007) *Guardianship Provision Systems for Unaccompanied and Separated Children Seeking Asylum in Europe, Initial Mapping.* Geneva: UNHCR.

Children's Rights Alliance for England (2008) *UK Implementation of the Convention on the Rights of the Child. NGO Alternative Report to the Committee on the Rights of the Child – ENGLAND.* London: CRAE.

Council of Europe (2005) *Convention on Action against Trafficking in Human Beings.* Warsaw: COE.

ECPAT UK (2010) *Guardianship for Child Victims of Trafficking.* London: ECPAT UK. Accessed on 31 October 2010 at www.ecpat.org.uk/sites/default/files/guardianship_briefing.pdf

ILPA (2006) *The Immigration Law Practitioners' Association's Evidence to the Joint Committee on Human Rights Inquiry into Treatment of Asylum Seekers.* London: ILPA.

House of Commons debates (2011) *Trafficking in Human Beings.* Accessed on 19 May 2011 at www.publications.parliament.uk/pa/cm201011/cmhansrd/cm110509/debtext/110509-0003.htm

Kohli, R. and Crawley, H. (2010) *Separated Children Guardianship in Scotland Pilot: First Interim Evaluation Report* (unpublished).

Refugee Children's Consortium (2007) *Response to the Home Office Consultation Paper Planning Better Outcomes and Support for Unaccompanied Asylum Seeking Children.* London. Accessed on 29 October 2010 at www.refugeecouncil.org.uk/OneStopCMS/Core/CrawlerResourceServer.aspx?resource=F5EC2788-F630-44DE-BF63-6901A39283D2&mode=link&guid=49f45671ff074e88a693f74041b7a73d

Save the Children UK (2008) *Guardianship for Separated Children in the UK: Stakeholder Views* (unpublished report).

Scottish Refugee Council and Aberlour Childcare Trust (2009) *Separated Children Guardianship in Scotland Pilot. Joint Business Plan* (unpublished).

Separated Children in Europe Programme (2008) *Statement of Good Practice. 4th Revised Edition.* First published 2004. Denmark: SCEP.

Sillen, J. and Beddoe, C. (2007) *Rights Here, Rights Now: Recommendations for Protecting Trafficked Children.* London: UNICEF UK, ECPAT UK.

The Anti-Trafficking Monitoring Group with Dottridge, M. (2010) *Wrong Kind of Victim. One Year On: An Analysis of UK Measures to Protect Trafficked Persons.* London: Anti-Slavery International for the Anti-Trafficking Monitoring Group.

The United Nations Children's Fund (2006) *Guidelines on the Protection of Child Victims of Trafficking, UNICEF Technical Notes.* New York: UNICEF.

UK Children's Commissioners (2008) *Report to the UN Committee on the Rights of the Child (2008), United Kingdom.* Accessed on 29/10/10 at www.sccyp.org.uk/downloadfileitem.aspx?file=2473

UK Government (2007) *The Consolidated 3rd and 4th Periodic Report to the UN Committee on the Rights of the Child.* Geneva: UNCRC.

UN Committee on the Rights of the Child (2002) *Thirty-First Session. Concluding Observations United Kingdom of Great Britain and Northern Ireland.* Geneva: UNCRC.

UN Committee on the Rights of the Child (2005) *Treatment of Unaccompanied and Separated Children outside their Country of Origin.* General Comment No. 6. Geneva: UNCRC.

UN Committee on the Rights of the Child (2008) *Forty-Ninth Session. Concluding Observations United Kingdom of Great Britain and Northern Ireland.* Geneva: UNCRC.

UN High Commissioner for Refugees (1997) Guidelines on Policies and Procedures in Dealing with Unaccompanied Children Seeking Asylum, February 1997. Accessed on 27 October 2010 at www.unhcr.org/refworld/docid/3ae6b3360.html

UN High Commissioner for Refugees (2008) *Guidelines on Determining the Best Interests of the Child.* Geneva: UNHCR.

UN High Commissioner High Commissioner for Refugees Representation to the United Kingdom in London (2009) *Quality Initiative Project. Sixth Report to the Minister.* London: UNHCR.

Vestegen, T. and Murk, J. (2010) *Towards a European Network of Guardianship Institutions.* Utrecht: Nidos Foundation and Refugium e.V.

Glossary

ADSS	Association of Directors of Social Services
BAAF	British Association for Adoption and Fostering
CEOP	Child Exploitation and Online Protection Centre
COE	Council of Europe Convention on Action against Trafficking in Human Beings 2005
CPS	Crown Prosecution Service
DCSF	Department for Children, Schools and Families
ECHR	European Convention for the Protection of Human Rights and Fundamental Freedoms
ECPAT UK	End Child Prostitution, Child Pornography and the Trafficking of Children for Sexual Purposes
EEA	European Economic Area
EPO	Emergency Protection Order
EU	European Union
ILPA	Immigration Law Practitioners' Association
IRO	Independent Reviewing Officer
LIT	Local Immigration Team
LSCB	Local Safeguarding Children Board
NAM	New Asylum Model
NASS	National Asylum Support Service
NCB	National Children's Bureau
NGO	Non-Governmental Organisation
NRM	National Referral Mechanism
NRUC	National Register for Unaccompanied Children

NSPCC	National Society for the Prevention of Cruelty to Children
PTSD	Post-traumatic stress disorder
SCCYP	Scotland's Commissioner for Children and Young People
SCEP	Separated Children in Europe Programme
SOCA	Serious Organised Crime Agency
UASC	Unaccompanied Asylum Seeking Child
UKBA	United Kingdom Border Agency
UKHTC	United Kingdom Human Trafficking Centre
UMT	Unaccompanied Minors Team
UNCRC	United Nations Convention on the Rights of the Child 1989
CRC	United Nations Committee on the Rights of the Child
UNHCR	United Nations High Commissioner for Refugees
YOI	Youth Offenders Institute
YOT	Youth Offending Team

List of Acts

Age of Legal Capacity (Scotland) Act 1991

Asylum and Immigration (Treatment of Claimants) Act 2004

Borders, Citizenship and Immigration Act 2009

Children Act 1989

Children Act 2004

Children (Leaving Care) Act 2000

Children (Northern Ireland) Order 1996

Children (Scotland) Act 1995

Children and Young Persons Act 2008

Citizenship and Immigration Act 2009

Criminal Justice (Scotland) Act 2003

Foster Children (Scotland) Act 1984

Human Rights Act 1998

Immigration and Asylum Act 1999

Nationality, Immigration and Asylum Act 2002

Sexual Offences Act 2003

UK Borders Act 2007

The Contributors

Farhat Bokhari is an independent consultant with an interest in migration, refugee, asylum seeking and trafficked children and women. Prior to consulting, she worked at ECPAT UK and raised the profile of child trafficking issues through research, writing and public speaking, contributing to a 20-country European anti-trafficking project and publishing a ground-breaking report on child trafficking for forced marriage while on fellowship with the University of Hull. As a researcher at Human Rights Watch, she documented and advocated against a wide range of human rights violations, particularly of the rights of refugees and trafficked children and women. She has extensive experience as an editor for web-based media covering human rights developments in the Asian and Middle Eastern region. She has published reports and articles on these subjects, most recently in *Child Slavery Now* (Policy Press 2010). She holds postgraduate and graduate degrees from the London School of Economics and is currently qualifying for a MSc in Social Work from the University of Bristol.

Heaven Crawley is Professor of International Migration and Director of the Centre for Migration Policy Research at Swansea University. She has undertaken research on asylum policy and practice in the UK and Europe since 1994, initially as part of a PhD at the University of Oxford and subsequently as head of asylum and immigration research at the UK Home Office and as associate director of the Institute for Public Policy Research. She has written and published extensively on a wide range of asylum and immigration issues including the impact of asylum policies, the interpretation of gendered experiences in the determination process, the causes of forced migration to Europe, public attitudes towards asylum and immigration issues and children's experiences of immigration controls, including detention. Her publications include *Guidelines for Best Practice on Working with Children Subject to Immigration Control* (ILPA 2004), *No Place for a Child: Children in UK Immigration Detention* (Save the Children 2005), *Child First, Migrant Second: Ensuring that Every Child Matters* (ILPA 2006), and *When is a Child not a Child? Asylum, Age Disputes and the Process of Age Assessment* (ILPA 2007).

Mina Fazel is a postdoctoral research fellow funded by the National Institute for Health Research. She is based in the Oxford University Department of Psychiatry and is an honorary consultant in child and adolescent psychiatry. Her research interests include developing mental health services for vulnerable populations, in particular refugee children.

Nadine Finch has practised as a barrister for nearly 20 years and is a member of Garden Court Chambers in London. She also sits as a fee paid immigration judge and provides expert advice to the family court at all levels. The practice involves the representation of children in immigration and asylum, community care and family courts. During the last year she has worked with and for UNHCR, UNICEF and the Children's Commissioner for England.

Philip Ishola has worked within the local and central government field of child protection and child and adult safeguarding for 15 years, extensively focused around safeguarding unaccompanied children and families seeking asylum seeking asylum in the UK. As part of these roles Philip has led the development of a range of care, integration and transition and safe returns polices, procedures and strategies incorporating a strong safeguarding focus. Philip currently chairs the London Safeguarding Children Board Trafficked Children National Monitoring Group and is chair of the London SCB 2012 Olympics (safe games for children) group which incorporates an advisory role on all safeguarding children matters (including child trafficking) to the Greater London Authority GLA 2012 Olympic Network. Philip is a member of the Association of Directors of Children Services National Asylum Task Force (for which he holds the counter child trafficking portfolio) and is also deputy chair of the UK Human Trafficking Centre (Serious Organised Crime Agency SOCA-HTC) Victim Care Group with specific responsibility for child welfare and is a member of the UK Government National Referral Mechanism Strategic Monitoring Group advising on safeguarding children matters. Philip is a strong advocate of the principle that the child's voice should be heard at all levels within agencies there to assist them.

Emma Kelly is a lecturer in social work (safeguarding children) at the University of Salford, teaching on the MA programme and leading the MSC in comparative safeguarding. She is a qualified social worker, with a background in child protection social work and interagency training for Manchester City Council. Since 2006 she has been interested in practitioner responses to child trafficking and held a UK-wide post on child trafficking training with ECPAT UK until 2009. She has published a number of chapters and articles on child trafficking, most recently in *Child Slavery Now* (Policy Press 2010).

Hannah Pearce was policy and advocacy manager at ECPAT UK between 2009 and 2011 working in particular on developing policy in response to child trafficking and lobbying parliament to better protect children's rights. Hannah previously worked for NGOs including Age Concern England, Breakthrough Breast Cancer and the British Institute of Human Rights in a range of campaigning roles. ECPAT UK is a leading children's rights organisation campaigning against the commercial sexual exploitation of children in the UK and on its international aspects. In particular, ECPAT UK focuses on the protection of children who have been trafficked and children exploited in tourism and the prevention of such crimes. ECPAT UK works through campaigning, research, training, policy development and legal reform.

Ruth Reed is a specialty registrar in Child and Adolescent Psychiatry in the Oxford School of Psychiatry. After qualifying as a doctor from Cambridge University, she trained in paediatrics followed by psychiatry, gaining experience in a variety of sub-specialties and settings in Glasgow, London and Oxford. She has a particular interest in the mental health of refugee children and parents.

Catherine Shaw is assistant director of the Research Centre at the National Children's Bureau (NCB). Prior to joining NCB she was a research fellow at the Policy Studies Institute and the Policy Research Bureau. Over the years her research and evaluation projects have covered a wide range of fields, although she is particularly interested in issues relating to vulnerable or marginalised children and young people. Catherine has a particular interest in evaluation, including supporting and training practitioners to evaluate their own projects and services. She is also interested in participatory approaches to research with children and young people. In 2009/10 she led a research project on private fostering commissioned by the Department for Children, Schools and Families (DCSF).

Savita de Sousa has responsibility for policy and development issues relating to private fostering and black minority ethnic children, who are unable to live with their birth parents at BAAF. Previously she has worked for local authorities and the voluntary sector. She has worked as a social worker, staff development officer and manager. She has experience of working in social care, corporate services and multidisciplinary teams. She has worked with black minority ethnic children and communities, disabled children and their families, support groups and the placement needs of children in adoption and fostering. Savita coordinates the BAAF Black Minority Ethnic Perspectives Advisory Committee (BMEPAC) and chairs the BAAF Private Fostering Special Interest Groups in England. As such, she is involved in all aspects of BAAF's work and has a national remit. She provides advice, information, consultancy and training. She develops links with other professionals and practitioners within the field of childcare to exchange views, share information and to work towards an improvement of the services offered to the black minority ethnic children and children in private foster care arrangements.

Stefan Stoyanov has a master's degree in Bulgarian and English Language and Literature and an MSc in European Social Policy. Stefan has been a children's rights advocate for over 15 years. He has worked in Bulgaria, England and Scotland in various policy, advocacy and campaigning roles with Save the Children UK, ECPAT UK and the NSPCC. He is currently a policy officer with Scotland's Commissioner for Children and Young People. His policy areas of expertise include deinstitutionalisation of child welfare systems, inter-country adoptions, asylum seeking children and child victims of trafficking.

Subject Index